PROSPER
AND BE IN
HEALTH

3ʳᵈ John 1.2

TOMMY COMBS

✝ Combs

Published by

LIFEBRIDGE
BOOKS
P.O. BOX 49428
CHARLOTTE, NC 28277

Printed in the United States of America.

CONTENTS

INTRODUCTION

There have been times in my ministry that God ordained a certain person to cross my path—or for a specific word of wisdom to be given to me. These moments have literally been life changing.

I believe with all my heart that the book you are about to read will be one of those turn-around experiences for you.

Why do I say this? Of all the verses in Scripture, the one we are about to discover affects the basics of your life—your success, your health, and your very soul.

I pray you will read and receive this with an open heart, saying, "Lord, what do You want me to receive from this? How can I apply this truth today and tomorrow?"

If you think this is a book just about money, you may be sorely disappointed, because in God's Kingdom, abundance applies to much more than our finances—yet it certainly includes that too.

FAVOR BEYOND MEASURE

For some, this will be a crash course in biblical

economics. For others it will open their eyes to the fact that God pays material, physical, and spiritual, dividends, both in this life and the one to come.

You will discover how to establish a covenant relationship with your heavenly Father that will bring favor beyond measure.

You'll learn:

- Three reasons God wants you to prosper
- The keys to a godly life
- Five principles that will unlock the floodgates of heaven
- God's plan for becoming debt free
- How to wage the battle for your healing
- The link between worship and wellness
- The requirements for receiving God's promises
- Ten steps to healing and health
- How to form a divine partnership with God
  – and much more.

Eternal Abundance

I have experienced the miraculous results of knowing, memorizing, speaking, and confessing God's Word when facing the circumstances of life. It is my earnest prayer that after reading this book you will also become "Word conscious." As a result, you will be able to take authority over every financial crisis, sickness, disease, or challenge you encounter.

Most important, you will learn how to receive spiritual prosperity—the only abundance that is eternal.

Get ready for your blessings to multiply. God wants you to prosper and be in health—even as your soul prospers.

— *Tommy Combs*

PART I

I PRAY THAT
YOU MAY PROSPER

CHAPTER 1

DESTINATION: PROSPERITY

From as young as I can remember, people were asking me, "What are you going to be when you grow up?"

It's part of childhood to dream about the future, but there comes a time when we need to ask ourselves, "What does God want me to be? What is His vision for my tomorrow?"

I have good news! The Lord has a destination in mind just for you—and it is detailed in Scripture.

One of the most powerful verses written in God's Word is the foundation for what you are about to discover: *"Beloved, I pray that you may prosper in all things and be in health, just as your soul prospers"* (3 John 1:2).

These are not just random thoughts of encouragement, rather it is a declaration that encompasses major areas of your life—your well being, your physical body, and your eternal soul.

Much of the New Testament was written by the apostles of old as helpful letters (called epistles) to individuals and churches. However, when we look at the book of 3 John, it is more like a postcard, rather than a letter. It's concise and short—just one chapter. Yet it is a profound revelation for you and me.

John is writing to his close friend, Gaius, a man who offered hospitality to the apostles and was dearly loved by John.

Let's read the first four verses: *"The Elder [John], to the beloved Gaius, whom I love in truth: Beloved, I pray that you may prosper in all things and be in health, just as your soul prospers. For I rejoiced greatly when brethren came and testified of the truth that is in you, just as you walk in the truth. I have no greater joy than to hear that my children walk in truth"* (3 John 1:1-4).

When we see concepts or ideas repeated in Scripture, we need to play close attention. Why? Because God does not mince or waste words.

In these four verses, three words are repeated at least twice: (1) love (beloved), (2) prosper, and (3) truth.

STANDING IN THE GAP

John is communicating to one person, yet there is a dual purpose. He is praying to God to help Gaius. At the same time, John is letting his friend know, "I love you, and because I do, here is what I am praying for on your behalf."

Stop and think for a moment. Who do you know right now who is talking to God about you? Of even more importance, who do you love enough to pray for? What individual means so much that you carve out the time to bombard heaven on their behalf—to stand in the gap for them?

In the original Greek construction of the previous text, the phrases are reversed, so it should be read, "Above all things, I pray that you may prosper." This was John's prayer.

MORE THAN MONEY

In the 21st century church, there are men and women who struggle with the very idea of prosperity. Because of some teaching, there are those who believe that acquiring wealth is the result of a "name it and claim it" process.

The enemy, Satan, has done an amazing job of distorting the biblical concept of prosperity. The devil wants us to think only about the preachers who unashamedly flaunt their luxurious lifestyles.

Prosperity, however, encompasses far more than just money and material possessions. We must never limit God regarding how He wants us to prosper.

Let's examine what the word "prosper" means. The root word denotes "a road, a way," or "a journey to travel."

In this context, to prosper means that we take the path God has planned for us—and we complete it successfully.

If you are embarking on a trip, there must be a destination or a destiny the Lord has called you to fulfill. If you are tuned into heaven you will hear God saying:

- "I speak success to your journey!"
- "I speak success to your calling!"
- "I speak success to your ministry!"
- "I speak success to your business!"
- "I speak success to your relationships!"
- "I speak success to your finances!"

Above all things, your heavenly Father desires that you prosper and succeed on your journey through this life and give Him all the honor and glory.

While financial blessings are part of prosperity,

there is so much more. As Christians we are not alone, stumbling blindly in the dark, because where God guides, He also provides.

WALKING IN TRUTH

I'm sure you have met people who have acquired all the money they will ever need, yet they are living an unfulfilled, miserable existence. They have unlimited cash in the bank, but they are emotionally bankrupt, searching for what riches cannot buy— longing for peace of mind, and a clean heart.

If God limited the definition of prosperity only to money, some of us would surely miss the boat!

Thank God, everything you need for your journey has been provided by your heavenly Father. Better yet, He has released His favor so we can walk in His promises.

The enemy tries his best to keep you talking about prosperity, yet never actually attaining it. He constantly whispers in your ear, "This will never happen for you."

Be strong in your faith and with boldness, block out his lies.

Your "walk" speaks about your lifestyle and your commitment. This is why John tells us that he is praying that we would live in truth.

Regardless of the miles to be traveled, this exciting adventure is taken step-by-step. As the apostle Paul wrote to the believers at Ephesus, *"We are His workmanship, created in Christ Jesus for good works, which God prepared beforehand that we should walk in them"* (Ephesians 2:10).

This tells us once more that this life is a journey the Lord arranged before we were ever born—and He wants us to complete it successfully.

WHAT IS YOUR ASSIGNMENT?

As you move forward, there are assigned tasks and stops you must make along the way. Yet, the Lord has already prepared for you to prosper in the process.

God has pre-ordained tasks for you to perform, and only when you complete them will your trip be rewarding.

Jesus understood this. He declared, *"I have glorified You on the earth. I have finished the work which You have given Me to do"* (John 17:4).

We glorify and honor God by completing the assignment He has given us to do.

You may question, "I don't know what my task is is."

God's Word makes our mission clear: *"Go...and make disciples of all the nations"* (Matthew 28:19).

16

These are our marching orders we must obey in order to glorify God.

A Day of Accounting

Please allow me to be totally honest. The church, for the most part, has done a good job in constructing buildings, adding members, forming choirs, arranging conferences, and detailing budgets, but what about making disciples? This is where we are weak!

It is so much easier to take the easy route and place an extra check in the offering plate when a missionary visits our church than to personally witness and evangelize.

There will come a day of accounting when God Almighty will say to so many: "You've been a failure. You did not run the course. You have not made disciples."

There are both corporate and personal responsibilities to be undertaken, but we must seek God's will for the right task for us personally.

If you were enrolled in a college course, what would be the benefit of turning in a project after the final exams were over? Many requirements are for a season, so there may be no value in doing what was needed last year.

God has a "now" work for you. Prayerfully seek His will, listen to His voice, and complete the task on schedule. There's little benefit in doing the "right stuff" at the wrong time.

WHY PROSPERITY?

I believe there are three major reasons God wants you to prosper, not only financially, but in every area of your life:

First, the Lord desires for you to be an example to others.

Your achievements are a living testimony to the world of what God can do through a person who is totally yielded to Him. It allows the Almighty to demonstrate His power and love.

It is written that *"God has chosen the foolish things of the world to put to shame the wise, and God has chosen the weak things of the world to put to shame the things which are mighty"* (1 Corinthians 1:27).

Second: The Lord wants you to provide for your family.

Scripture is clear on this point: *"If anyone does not*

provide for his own, and especially for those of his household, he has denied the faith and is worse than an unbeliever" (1 Timothy 5:8).

God never intended for you to live the life of a beggar. As the psalmist wrote, *"I have been young, and now am old; yet I have not seen the righteous forsaken, nor his descendants begging bread"* (Psalm 37:25).

We serve a God who is a provider, and He expects no less of us.

Third: Being prosperous allows you to help carry out the Great Commission.

It takes prayer, work, and finances to build strong churches and spread the Gospel to the unsaved. I believe God wants to bless His children with abundant resources so they are able to be joyful givers to His Kingdom.

YOUR DESTINATION

God has an ultimate objective for each of us and that destination is prosperity! He desires for every corner of our lives to prosper—our emotions, our physical body, and our soul. God wants us to flourish in our marriage, our ministry, and our mind. Yes, we are to rise to the top in all we do.

The Lord has already completed His part in making this happen. His Kingdom is available, but it is up to us to line up with His plan and purpose.

Let me share eight steps to making sure you reach the destination of prosperity:

Step #1: Receive the Word of God.

This is where the process begins. The Word is the "incorruptible seed" (1 Peter 2:3) that always produces and never fails.

His Word is the origin—the doorway—for all prosperity, and without it you will never fulfill the Father's vision for your future. It is your revelation from the Almighty.

Prosperity is Word-determined. This "Word seed" will cause you to succeed when the doubters and critics says there is no way. It will prosper your marriage when a counselor suggests divorce. It will heal your mind when the psychiatrist recommends a mental hospital.

Step #2: Let God control your thought life.

Our thoughts are "things" that have power over our mind and behavior. The Bible tells us, *"As [a man] thinks in his heart, so is he"* (Proverbs 23:7).

What many are told as a child is true: if you think you are a failure you will be a failure. On the other hand, if you think you will be an achiever, this is what you will become.

In the final analysis "Word" thinking is prosperity thinking. So let your mind be filled and controlled by God through His precious Word.

Step #3: Ask the Lord to take charge of your emotions.

When your thinking is in accord with the Word of God, your feelings will be too. Emotions can be aroused by pain or pleasure and swayed in one direction or another.

We cannot ignore the fact that the Lord created us as an emotional being. As such, we must treat this as a gift from our heavenly Father. In fact, Jesus had emotions. He cried and was touched by compassion. For this reason He can *"sympathize with our weaknesses"* (Hebrews 4:15).

It is human nature to have emotions, but never let your emotions have you!

We must learn to take authority over our feelings. In the Garden of Gethsemane, just before He would be betrayed, Jesus said to His disciples, "'Sit here while

I pray.' And He took Peter, James, and John with Him, and He began to be troubled and deeply distressed" (Mark 14:34).

At the time of His greatest need, Jesus prayed.

Regardless of what you are going through, God can speak peace to your heart through prayer.

Step #4: Find God's will for your decisions.

Everyday living presents us with a never-ending series of choices and options. God has created us as free moral agents and has given us the power to choose. The Lord declares, "*I call heaven and earth as witnesses today against you, that I have set before you life and death, blessing and cursing; therefore choose life, that both you and your descendants may live*" (Deuteronomy 30:19).

This is why we need to come before God and make certain that our choices are in His perfect will.

I love the story of a man named Jairus, a ruler of the synagogue, who made a decision to get the attention of Jesus. Scripture records that *"when he saw Him he fell at His feet and begged Him earnestly, saying, 'My little daughter lies at the point of death. Come and lay Your hands on her, that she may be healed, and she will live'"* (Mark 5:22-23).

Right in the middle of this encounter, another

decision was being made. A woman with an issue of blood arrived on the scene, determined to touch Jesus. She believed, *"If only I may touch His clothes, I shall be made well"* (verse 28). And that's exactly what she did. As a result, the woman was totally healed.

Jesus then went with Jairus to the bedside of his ailing daughter, who had now been pronounced dead. But the Son of God declared, *"The child is not dead, but sleeping"* (verse 39), He took her by the hand and said, *"Arise,"* (verse 41) and she awoke and walked.

Both of these were miracles that began with a decision.

When your determination parallels God's will, Jesus will stop for you, He will come to your house—to you and your family. The burdens will be lifted; the enemy will be destroyed.

Step #5: Act on what you believe.

Your decisions determine your actions and your actions cause your faith to increase. So begin to act on what you believe. As the apostle Paul said, *"This one thing I do"* (Philippians 3:13).

Jesus didn't tell us to just pray about spreading the Word, He commanded, *"Go into all the world and preach the gospel to every creature"* (Mark 16:15).

23

The key word here is the verb, "Go!"

Remember, "*Faith without works is dead*" (James 2:26).

Stop procrastinating. Get up and get moving! Let your actions demonstrate what you believe.

Step #6: Pray that your habits will line up with God's Word.

Your actions will determine your habits. What you repeat, over and over again on a daily basis, becomes so ingrained on your mind, that eventually it is automatic. If you lie repeatedly, it will become a destructive pattern. If you overeat constantly, it will dominate your behavior until it becomes a health threat.

Make your habits work for you instead of against you. For example, set a time every day for reading and studying God's Word. Stay with your commitment and it will soon become the best habit you ever acquired. I guarantee that you'll be changed from the inside out.

Since your potential is wrapped up in your habits, with God's help take charge of them—today, tomorrow, and as long as you live.

Step #7: Guard your character.

Your habits will produce your character—the qualities people come to expect from you.

Since you will never rise above the limitations of your character, make a vow to God that you will do what is right—just because it is right.

Use Jesus as your example. He walked this earth and demonstrated love, compassion, and truth.

Step #8: Expect the blessings of God.

I believe you now understand how all of this weaves together. The Word of God controls your thoughts; your thoughts control you emotions; your emotions affect your decisions; your decisions affect your actions; your actions determine your habits; and your habits determine your character.

When all of these areas are in proper alignment with God's Word, you can expect the blessing and favor of heaven to be yours.

Your destiny has been determined: you are to prosper in every way!

It Pays to Live for the Lord

In these times of uncertainty and chaos it is comforting to know that we serve an unchanging Jehovah who is dependable. What an assurance!

Without question, it pays to live a godly life. As Scripture teaches, *"Godliness is profitable for all things, having promise of the life that now is and of that which is to come"* (1 Timothy 4:8).

Here, Paul is writing about what it means to live for the Lord today—and how it affects your eternity.

There are individuals who believe that living for God doesn't pay dividends in this life. They need to reevaluate! This verse tells us we are to be profitable *now!*

It's easy to talk about a heaven with no more tears and no more failures, but God promises us blessings in this life on earth.

He has made an investment in you and me—and expects it to produce a healthy profit.

We live a life pleasing to God by following the counsel of the apostle: *"To but be an example to the believers in word, in conduct, in love, in spirit, in faith, in purity"* (verse 12).

Now this is profitable living!

THE GODLY LIFE

Today, *"Do not neglect the gift that is in you ...Meditate on these things; give yourself entirely to them, that your progress may be evident to all. Take heed to yourself and to the doctrine. Continue in them, for in doing this you will save both yourself and those who hear you"* (verses 14-16).

The Lord not only welcomes us into His family, but also wants us to bring glory to His name. When we do, it produces a return on His investment.

There are awesome benefits to leading a godly life:

1. Godliness gives you protection.

We have a loving, caring Father, and if you are His and He is yours, you can expect Him to take care of you. After all, *"You were bought at a price; therefore glorify God in your body and in your spirit, which are God's"* (1 Corinthians 6:20).

The apostle Paul certainly knew who he belonged to. As a result, the Lord protected him. Through hardships, brutal beatings, and imprisonment, there was always divine protection.

As a captive on his way to Rome to stand before the judgment of Caesar, the ship he was sailing on was ripped to pieces on the jagged rocks. But Paul had the assurance that God was watching over him: *"For there stood by me this night an angel of the God to whom I belong and whom I serve"* (Acts 27:23).

There was no doubt who was protecting him: the One he served!

Two: Godliness leads to prosperity.

I have seen the Lord work financial miracles in the lives of many businessmen and women who built their enterprises on the biblical principle of tithing and giving offerings.

Money is not ours to hoard or keep. It all belongs to the Creator and He allows us to use it for a short while on this earth.

I've been asked, "Do you tithe on what is left after you have paid all your bills?"

No, the Bible tells us we are to give God a tenth of the "first fruits"—this means before we spend one penny on anything else. *"Honor the Lord with your possessions, and with the firstfruits of all your increase"* (Proverbs 3:9).

When you pay God first, He will bless you so abundantly that your storehouse will not be able to contain the overflow (Malachi 3:10).

Living a godly life in obedience to Him brings divine prosperity.

Three: Godliness results in promotion.

The greatest advancement you will ever experience will be yours when you enter eternity as a result of asking Jesus to be your Lord and Savior and living the Christ-like life.

The Bible tells us, *"He who overcomes shall inherit all things"* (Revelation 21:7). We are also told, *"Blessed are those who do His commandments, that they may have the right to the tree of life, and may enter through the gates into the city"* (Revelation 22:14).

What a glorious time of celebration that will be!

Chapter 2

It's a Promise!

If God says He will do something for you, you can take it to the bank!

We covet God's promises, but there are certain things we are required to do in order to receive them.

Look at the life of Abraham. God told him, *"You shall be a father of many nations"* (Genesis 17:4).

To be specific, God said, *"I will multiply your descendants as the stars of the heaven and as the sand which is on the seashore...In your seed all the nations of the earth shall be blessed"* (Genesis 22:17-18).

How was this prophecy possible? Sarah, Abraham's wife, was barren and past childbearing age. Yet the Lord made it clear that his lineage would not come from a surrogate, but through Sarah.

Despite this, did Abraham doubt God? Not for one moment. Scripture tells us, *"And being not weak in faith, he considered not his own body now dead, when he was about an hundred years old, neither yet the deadness of Sarah's womb: he staggered not at the promise of God through unbelief; but was strong in faith, giving glory to God; and being fully persuaded that, what he had promised, he was able also to perform"* (Romans 4:19-21 KJV).

This marvelous passage reveals the steps Abraham followed in order to see God's promises fulfilled.

First: Abraham had a strong faith.

The Bible records, *"The promise that he should be the heir for the promise, that he should be the heir of the world, was not to Abraham, or to his seed, through the law, but through the righteousness of faith"* (Romans 4:13).

His belief was unshakable.

Second: Abraham ignored the natural circumstances.

Abraham *"considered not"* the fact that Sarah was too old to conceive and carry a child. Instead of relying on the natural process of life—consider the *super*natural. God operates in a realm that is extraordinary.

Third: Abraham believed the promises of God.

He *"staggered not"* through unbelief, but by faith placed His trust in what the Lord said.

When you believe God with all your mind, heart, and soul, you will begin to receive His promises for you.

In the New Testament, James gives this advice: *"Let him ask in faith, with no doubting, for he who doubts is like a wave of the sea driven and tossed by the wind. For let not that man suppose that he will receive anything from the Lord; he is a double-minded man, unstable in all his ways"* (James 1:6-8).

Abraham was *"fully persuaded"* and totally convinced that God would honor His covenant.

Stop doubting and start believing!

Fourth: Abraham thanked God for the answer in advance.

It is significant to note that Abraham offered *"glory to God"* (Romans 4:20) before any of the promises were a reality.

This is a biblical principle we all should practice every time we call on God. Thank Him for the answer *in advance!* The Bible tells us, *"Be anxious for nothing, but in everything by prayer and supplication, with thanksgiving, let your requests be made known to God"* (Philippians 4:6).

In expectation, give thanks for the answer at the time you make your petition.

FRIGHTENED BY THE WAVES

I see men and women in an anointed service who become sky high spiritually. Then after a few days, their faith seems to waver, they start concentrating on their circumstances more than their belief in God.

Satan targets believers with doubts, "You can't. You won't. You'd better not try." He tries to sabotage your spirit and wants you to stagger at the prospect of failure.

It was the enemy who attacked the faith of the apostle Peter when he tried to walk on the water toward Jesus.

Do you remember the scene? The disciples were out on the sea of Galilee at night when a great storm came out of nowhere. They were frightened, but walking toward them on the turbulent waves was Jesus, who said, *"It is I; do not be afraid"* (Matthew 14:27).

Peter responded, *"Lord, if it is You, command me to come to You on the water"* (verse 28).

At the invitation of Jesus, Peter climbed out of the

boat and began to walk toward the Lord.

Then it happened. The enemy planted seeds of doubt, and Peter took his eyes off of Jesus and looked at the storm and the waves. The Bible records that *"He was afraid; and beginning to sink he cried out, saying, 'Lord, save me!'"* (verse 30).

Immediately, Jesus reached out His hand and rescued Peter.

I pray you will choose to keep your eyes focused on the Master and believe the promises of our heavenly Father.

THE ULTIMATE TEST

Abraham had no doubt that he served a promise-fulfilling God. This is why he did not flinch when the Almighty asked him to take his promised son, Isaac, to the mountain and offer him as a sacrifice.

This father of faith was persuaded that even if he obeyed, somehow God would bring back his son.

The mighty faith of Abraham was so evident, that at the last moment, with Isaac bound and laid on the altar, as he was about to bring down the knife to slay his son, an angel of the Lord called down from heaven: "Abraham, Abraham." He answered, *"Here I am"* (Genesis 22:11).

God's messenger ordered, *"Do not lay your hand*

on the lad, or do anything to him; for now I know that you fear God, since you have not withheld your son, your only son, from Me" (verse 12).

When Abraham turned to look, he saw a ram caught in a thicket by his horns. It became the sacrificial offering.

With gratitude in his heart he named the place, "The Lord Will Provide."

Do We Really Believe?

Down through the years many fathers have told their sons: "If you make good grades and show me you are responsible, when you turn sixteen, I am going to buy you a car."

The young man looks forward to that day with more than anticipation. He dreams about cruising around town in his own automobile. He doesn't have the keys yet but he has faith and belief in his dad.

The special birthday finally arrives and his father doesn't let him down. It is a promise kept.

If we can have such faith and trust in our earthly father, why do we doubt our heavenly Father?

There are church member who avoid talking about what God can do for them. Why? Because they are not fully convinced of the Lord's power. There's doubt in their voice and you can sense their uncertainty by listening to their faltering words.

It is time for each of us to return to the faith of Abraham and be fully persuaded that what God promises He will provide.

TURN OFF THE ALARM!

We live in a world where alarms are going off constantly. Millions wake up every morning to the sound of an alarm—and some people hear them ringing throughout the day. Perhaps you know a friend who sets an alarm for certain times as a reminder of an important phone call or to take prescription medicine.

Alarms are used to alert us to important or dangerous situations. For example, hospitals use machines to monitor patients, and when a person or a piece of equipment needs special attention, an alarm alerts the medical personnel on duty. Every military base is equipped with alarms to warn of an impending enemy attack.

Perhaps you live in a community with sirens that are triggered when there is a violent storm or tornado approaching. And we equip our homes with smoke and radon detectors that emit a screeching sound when fire or gas is detected.

There are times in our personal lives when we face problems so great that a warning signal explodes in our mind. When this happens, instead of reacting like trained doctors, firemen, or soldiers, we tend to get overly excited and panic. Some people run around in circles, not knowing what on earth to do.

Let's face it. Satan is working overtime, trying to push God's people into a panic mode. However, there is a way to find calm in the midst of the storm—to turn off the alarm.

A PLACE OF SAFETY

The next time you sense danger, start quoting the promises of God's Word. In your moment of distress, begin to say, *"God is our refuge and strength, a very present help in trouble"* (Psalm 46:1).

If you are at home, school, or place of business, when the fire alarm sounds you look for a place of safety. In the spiritual world, the same principle applies. Start running toward your refuge—the arms of your heavenly Father. He is your ultimate protection.

Far too often, when the enemy attacks, we cave in and allow our weakness to take over, saying to ourselves,"I can't handle this!"

Well, you may not have the strength or fortitude, but I know One who does. Hear the promise of the Father, *"Fear not, for I am with you; be not dismayed, for I am your God. I will strengthen you, yes, I will help you, I will uphold you with My righteous right hand"* (Isaiah 41:10).

It seems that some people can read the promises of God again and again, yet when panic strikes, they fail to act on the Word. Instead, they give way to anxiety and frustration.

After telling us that God is our refuge, our strength, and a very present help in trouble, the psalmist concludes, *"Therefore we will not fear"* (Psalm 46:2).

Fear is a major tool Satan uses to ruin our relationship with the Lord.

It is foolish to drive 80 or 90 miles an hour down a dirt road and brag, "I have no fear. The Lord is my protection. He will take care of me." How foolish. This is tempting God rather than using common sense.

Whoever you are, and wherever you go, the Lord is forever by your side. No matter how black the clouds may be, He is in the middle of the storm. So rest in His peace.

WHAT POWER!

Psalm 46 details God's intervention in the lives of the children of Israel. We are told how *"the nations raged, the kingdoms were moved; He uttered His voice, the earth melted"* (verse 6). What power!

At the voice of God, your problems too can melt away.

Perhaps you doubt and say, "But the Lord hasn't spoken to me." Yes, He has. Jesus promised, *"If you can believe, all things are possible"* (Mark 9:23).

Not only has the Lord spoken in the past, but He is still speaking today. His Word is dependable. Read it. Remember it. Hide it in your heart and act upon it. God's Word is truth and the truth will set you free.

When trouble appears, let the written Word speak to the situation.

God gives us an invitation to see what He has done: *"Come, behold the works of the Lord,"* (Psalm 46:8). He has already defeated our enemy, so why should we continue to fear?

The vivid accounts of the children of Israel are lessons we must never ignore. They went to battle against all odds, always outnumbered and outmaneuvered. Yet, because God was on their side, there was victory.

In the final analysis, regardless of the circumstances and when everything around us is in chaos, the Father tells us, *"Be still, and know that I am God"* (Psalm 46:10). Today, enjoy His perfect peace.

YOU HAVE HELP

When you have done all you can do; when you've struggled and are bone-tired, the Lord is standing beside you and waiting for you to call on His name. At that moment He will lift you up and help carry your burden. In addition, He will give you knowledge and wisdom to face any situation.

God is in control. You're not going under—you are going over!

Where do you turn when you are trying to carry a load that is far too heavy? You ask for someone strong to help you. Today, I am thrilled to know that the Holy Spirit was sent to be my Helper.

Before Jesus returned to heaven, He gave us this assurance, *"I will pray the Father, and He will give you another Helper, that He may abide with you forever"* (John 14:16). He explained, *"The Helper, the Holy Spirit, whom the Father will send in My name, He will teach you all things"* (verse 26).

Turn off the alarm! You are safe and secure. Rest in Him.

PLANTING THE PROMISES

Are you aware that you are God's garden? He

created you as a field to be planted and His plan for you was established at the beginning of creation.

We know that every plot of land belongs to its owner. And since we were bought with a price, God holds the title and the deed to us.

We are totally His. We belong to Him by right of creation, by right of preservation, and by right of redemption.

This is not a problem, but a privilege. *"Do you not know that your body is the temple of the Holy Spirit who is in you, whom you have from God, and you are not your own? For you were bought at a price; therefore glorify God in your body and in your spirit, which are God's"* (1 Corinthians 6:19-20).

Since we are God's garden, how can we cultivate the soil so the promises of the Father will be active in our lives?

Most of us have read the Bible and we know what God's Word says, but how do we ensure that those promises will be fulfilled in us?

WHO GIVES THE INCREASE?

Since *"you are God's field"* (1 Corinthians 3:9), you must understand what a field is for. It is for planting seed, cultivating the plants, and reaping a harvest.

The apostle Paul explained how we, as God's

children, are to work in unity as we plant. He told the believers at Corinth, *"I planted, Apollos watered, but God gave the increase. So then neither he who plants is anything, nor he who waters, but God who gives the increase. Now he who plants and he who waters are one, and each one will receive his own reward according to his own labor. For we are God's fellow workers"* (1 Corinthians 3:6-9).

The Lord brings about His bountiful harvest in the same way a farmer does—by planting seeds.

THE SOWER

One day, on the shores of Galilee, a large crowd gathered around Jesus as He shared the Parable of the Sower.

He told the story of a man who went out to sow and as he did, some seed fell by the wayside and the birds came and devoured it. Some landed on stony ground: it sprang up but died immediately because the sun was hot and the roots were shallow. Other seed fell among thorns, but as it grew, it was choked out by the thorns themselves.

Jesus concluded by saying, *"But other seed fell on good ground and yielded a crop that sprang up, increased and produced: some thirtyfold, some sixty, and some a hundred"* (Mark 4:8).

When the crowd had departed, the disciples gathered around Jesus, still curious, and asked Him to explain the parable. Here's what the Lord told them:

The sower sows the word. And these are the ones by the wayside where the word is sown. When they hear, Satan comes immediately and takes away the word that was sown in their hearts.

These likewise are the ones sown on stony ground who, when they hear the word, immediately receive it with gladness; and they have no root in themselves, and so endure only for a time. Afterward, when tribulation or persecution arises for the word's sake, immediately they stumble.

Now these are the ones sown among thorns; they are the ones who hear the word, and the cares of this world, the deceitfulness of riches, and the desires for other things entering in choke the word, and it becomes unfruitful.

But these are the ones sown on good ground, those who hear the word, accept it, and bear fruit: some thirtyfold, some sixty, and some a hundred (Mark 4:14-20).

In a nutshell, the seed is the Word of God.

ACTIVATE THE SEED

Our heavenly Father has promised us many things—abundance, hope, joy, grace, mercy, strength, safety, peace, power, protection, provision, redemption, wisdom—the list is practically endless.

Here's the most important part. Every promise of God is based on our obedience to His Word. When it is planted in faith, the results are beyond amazing.

The seed, however, does no good until it is planted. Packed in a sack or stored in a bin, the seed is inactive; only when it is placed in the ground, watered and nourished does it spring alive and begin to sprout.

It is the same with God's Word. It is dormant until it is planted inside us. This is why the psalmist said, *"Your word I have hidden in my heart, that I might not sin against You"* (Psalm 119:11).

Many believers have memorized Scripture in their head, but it never reached their heart. Then they wonder why they are not producing fruit.

DEEP INSIDE

All of the wonderful works of God have their potential in His seed. As David explains, *"The word of*

45

the Lord is right, and all His work is done in truth."
(Psalm 33:4)

When Scripture permeates your spirit, all things are possible. Jesus said, *"If you abide in Me, and My words abide in you, you will ask what you desire, and it shall be done for you"* (John 15:7).

The moment the Word is planted in the soil of your heart, you truly begin to live. *"My son, give attention to my words; Incline your ear to my sayings. Do not let them depart from your eyes; keep them in the midst of your heart; for they are life to those who find them, and health to all their flesh"* (Proverbs 4:20-22).

Long ago I discovered this wonderful truth and began to carefully and prayerfully plant His seed into my heart. A bird didn't just fly overhead and drop faith into me. No, I deliberately read, spoke, memorized, and internalized verse after verse and tucked each one into my spirit.

Then I watered, cultivated, and nourished the Word until God Himself was living within me. From that time forward, every decision I have made and every promise I have claimed has come from this glorious Word. Praise the Lord!

PRECIOUS PROMISES

We are talking about treasures beyond compare.

The apostle Peter tells us we have been given *"exceedingly great and precious promises, that through these you may be partakers of the divine nature"* (2 Peter 1:4).

As seeds, these promises accomplish their marvelous work anytime they are planted in the soil God has given you.

It's up to you what will grow in your garden. What kind of seed have you been planting?

CHAPTER 3

NO MORE FAMINE!

It breaks my heart when I see the reports of hundreds of thousands of people dying of hunger and thirst in drought-stricken areas of Ethiopia, Sudan, and other African nations.

Because of crop failure, overpopulation, weather conditions, and sometimes even government policies, our fragile world is often thrown into disaster. The results are malnutrition, starvation, epidemics, and increased mortality.

It also troubles me when I see God's people living in spiritual famine. Their souls are parched, their spirits are thirsting, and their churches are dry. This is not what the Creator planned for His people.

The theme of this book is the bedrock principle and the bottom line for every believer: God wants you to prosper and be in health, even as your soul prospers.

Almighty God did not create you to live in a

wasteland. He has a plan for you that is far better.

As the psalmist wrote, *"He turns a wilderness into pools of water, and dry land into watersprings. There He makes the hungry dwell, that they may establish a city for a dwelling place, and sow fields and plant vineyards, that they may yield a fruitful harvest. He also blesses them, and they multiply greatly"* (Psalm 107:35-38).

Are you ready to say goodbye to your dry place and step into the rain? Wet ground becomes a fertile environment for crops to grow and thrive. It's the key to your harvest.

I believe God is ready to send a downpour of abundance on your physical, mental, emotional, and spiritual life.

The Lord says, *"I will call for the grain and multiply it, and bring no famine upon you. And I will multiply the fruit of your trees and the increase of your fields, so that you need never again bear the reproach of famine among the nations"* (Ezekiel 36:28-30).

This describes a world where God's Word is preached, people repent of their sins, and those who hunger and thirst after righteousness are fed and satisfied.

UNLOCK THE FLOODGATES

I want to share some principles that will unlock the

floodgates of heaven and cause you to receive the refreshing waters of God's Holy Spirit.

Principle #1: Your Seed is Sanctified

In order for you to prosper, God offers you springs of water that have His blessing, and the seed He has given you to sow has been sanctified from above.

It is your heavenly Father who provides for those who are thirsting. He promises, *"I will open rivers in desolate heights, and fountains in the midst of the valleys; I will make the wilderness a pool of water, and the dry land springs of water"* (Isaiah 41:18).

The Lord will prepare your soil, but what you bring to Him is also significant. Remember the question God asked Moses, *"What is that in your hand?"* (Exodus 4:2).

In the story of Cain and Abel, both gave an offering to the Lord, but Cain's was not accepted because it did not meet God's standards.

We must give the Lord seed that is sanctified and holy.

Principle #2: Sow Your Seed Regardless of the Circumstances

One day, when Jesus was in the temple, He saw

people putting money into the treasury. There were those who were wealthy and gave a substantial sum. Then one poor widow came along and threw in two "mites." These were the smallest monetary coins in Israel during that time.

When Jesus witnessed this, He gathered His disciples around Him and commented, *"Assuredly, I say to you that this poor widow has put in more than all those who have given to the treasury; for they all put in out of their abundance, but she out of her poverty put in all that she had, her whole livelihood"* (Mark 12:43-44).

It is not the size of the gift you present, but the sacrifice it represents.

Principle #3: Your Gift to God Must be Spotless

When God in heaven made the decision to offer the ultimate sacrifice for the sins of the world, He sent the best Had—His only Son. Jesus was *"a lamb without blemish and without spot"* (1 Peter 1:19).

He expects no less of you and me. The Lord is not looking for our leftovers, what we can do without, but the finest offering we can give.

God is jealous of our love and demands, *"You shall have no other gods before Me"* (Exodus 20:3). This tells us that anything we esteem above the Almighty is an idol that He will not accept.

Make certain what you present to the Lord is spotless and pure.

Principle #4: You Must Obey God's Commandments

In the days of the prophet Elisha there was a commander in the army of the king of Syria named Naaman. He was also afflicted with leprosy.

The commander's wife had heard about a man of God in Israel who could pray and believe for miracles.

Naaman, with his horses and chariots, arrived at the door of Elisha and was given this command: *"Go and wash in the Jordan seven times, and your flesh shall be restored to you, and you shall be clean"* (2 Kings 5:10).

Naaman thought this was a crazy idea, yet he did as he was told, with amazing results. The Bible gives this account: *"His flesh was restored like the flesh of a little child, and he was clean"* (verse 14).

To receive miracles in your life, obey the commands of the Lord when He speaks to you. God's timing is perfect.

Principle #5: Sow Your Seed in Good Soil

This step is vital. Make sure you are giving to a

church or ministry that presents God's Word without compromise—where salvation is preached and the gifts of the Spirit are in operation.

Avoid planting in undernourished, unsanctified soil.

We are living in the last days and the prophecy of Joel is at hand: *"He has given you the former rain faithfully, and He will cause the rain to come down for you—the former rain, and the latter rain"* (Joel 2:23).

Praise God, it's beginning to rain!

I pray you will follow these principles and allow the refreshing, restoring, and renewing power of God to flood you life. No more famine!

AN OFFERING OF FAITH

Let me ask a personal question. Have you ever participated in an "Offering of Faith"?

If you are wondering what that means, it is a pledge you make to God that you don't have any idea how it will be fulfilled. If you can afford the amount it is not a faith offering.

The results of such giving are mind-boggling. Only God Almighty can take our nothing and turn it into a miracle.

There was a widow woman in the days of the prophet Elijah who gave one of the greatest faith offerings ever recorded.

In a time of devastating famine, God instructed Elijah to go to a place called Zarephath. He was also told, *"I have commanded a widow there to provide for you"* (1 Kings 17:9).

When he arrived at the gates of the city, a widow was waiting, gathering sticks. Elijah called out to her and asked her to bring him a cup of water and a morsel of bread.

The woman responded, *"As the Lord your God lives, I do not have bread, only a handful of flour in a bin, and a little oil in a jar; and see, I am gathering a couple of sticks that I may go in and prepare it for myself and my son, that we may eat it, and die"* (verse 12).

Today, in the average American home, you can look in the pantry or the freezer and find enough food to last for weeks, but this woman was down to her last rations.

Yet, God told her in advance that a prophet would be coming and that she was to feed him.

Now if Elijah had asked for a warm blanket or a bed in which to sleep, she could have easily provided those things. But food? This request seemed impossible.

Elijah said to her, *"Do not fear; go and do as you have said, but make me a small cake from it first, and bring it to me; and afterward make some for yourself and your son"* (verse 13).

Have you ever given something away and had absolutely nothing left? Have you ever made a pledge and you didn't know where the resources were coming from? If so, then you know that this woman was giving an offering of faith.

Elisha also gave the widow a prophecy from God: *"The bin of flour shall not be used up, nor shall the jar of oil run dry, until the day the Lord sends rain on the earth"* (verse 14).

The woman did what she was told and a miracle unfolded before their eyes. The flour bin remained full and the vessel of oil did not diminish. Elijah, the widow, and her son were sustained by the hand of God.

If the Lord places it upon your heart to give—and it's more than you can afford—don't hesitate. Make an offering of faith and watch God begin to work.

YOUR PROVIDER

There are many Hebrew names for God, and each of them have special meaning. For example, He is El Shaddai (God All Sufficient), Jehovah Nissi (The Lord Our Banner), and Jehovah Shalom (The Lord our Peace).

Earlier, we recounted the story of Abraham offering

his son, Isaac, as a sacrifice. When God provided a ram to take his place, to Abraham, God was "Jehovah Jireh" (God our Provider).

These names were not just temporary, just for a few days or a certain period of time. God is all powerful. He says, *"I am the Lord, I do not change"* (Malachi 3:6).

I've heard the expression many times that "a person's name is only as good as their word." This is certainly true of our heavenly Father. His Word is His bond—and is bonded to His promises. As Jesus explained, *"Heaven and earth will pass away, but My words will by no means pass away"* (Matthew 24:35).

The Bible tells us, *"When God made a promise to Abraham, because He could swear by no one greater, He swore by Himself"* (Hebrews 6:13).

Think what would happen if the Father broke His covenant—He would destroy Himself and His Word.

In both the Old and New Testaments, Jehovah revealed that every blessing we receive is because of the covenant. He tells us over and over again that if we obey His commands we will be favored and blessed.

Today, you can stand on this assurance: *"My God shall supply all your need according to His riches in glory by Christ Jesus"* (Philippians 4:19).

He is our Jehovah Jireh—our Provider.

Ask in Jesus' Name

I cannot count how many sermons I have heard on the theme of "Asking and Receiving." It is a biblical principle, however, many well-meaning people leave out the one ingredient that is necessary if we expect our prayers to be answered.

What is the missing link? Our petitions to God must be asked in the name of Jesus.

Look closely what the Son of God taught on the subject: *"Whatever you ask in My name, that I will do, that the Father may be glorified in the Son. If you ask anything in My name, I will do it"* (John 14:13-14). And *"Whatever you ask the Father in My name He will give you"* (John 15:16).

I was ministering in the rainforest city of Iquitos, Peru, and had the privilege of praying for five deaf and dumb children. I did nothing except repeat the name of Jesus over and over again. One by one, ears were opened and they all began to hear. Then they began to speak—and each one uttered the name, "Jesus!"

Oh, what miracles we witnessed that day!

Above Every Name

At the gate of the temple, Peter saw a beggar who

had been lame from birth. With compassion, he told the man, *"Silver and gold I do not have, but what I do have I give you: In the name of Jesus Christ of Nazareth, rise up and walk"* (Acts 3:6).

The beggar was instantly healed.

Peter did not anoint the man with oil or lay hands on him. The healing was simply in Jesus' name.

In the city of Philippi, the apostle Paul encountered a young woman who was demon possessed. According to Scripture, Paul *"said to the spirit, 'I command you in the name of Jesus Christ to come out of her.' And he came out that very hour"* (Acts 16:18).

When Jesus gave us the right to use His name, God the Father knew all that would imply. We are able to minister with the signs and wonders promised to those who believe. *All* things are possible when we agree His name in prayer.

God has *"highly exalted Him and given Him the name which is above every name, that at the name of Jesus every knee should bow, of those in heaven, and of those on earth, and of those under the earth, and that every tongue should confess that Jesus Christ is Lord, to the glory of God the Father"* (Philippians 2:9-11).

This mean that Jesus holds dominion over men, angels, and demons—and all must bow to Him.

Whatever You Need

The possibilities are beyond our understanding when we use His wonderful name—in our thanks, in our praise, for *all* things.

- *"[Give] thanks always for all things to God the Father in the name of our Lord Jesus Christ"* (Ephesians 5:20).

- *"Let us continually offer the sacrifice of praise to God, that is, the fruit of our lips, giving thanks to His name"* (Hebrews 13:15).

- *"These things I have written to you who believe in the name of the Son of God, that you may know that you have eternal life, and that you may continue to believe in the name of the Son of God"* (1 John 5:13).

- *"Whatever you do in word or deed, do all in the name of the Lord Jesus"* (Colossians 3:17).

When Jesus says "whatever you ask in My name" He is handing you a blank check that bears His signature. This gives us the right to fill in the check—"whatever" the need, "whatever" the amount.

It has already been endorsed and all we have to do is write the date, fill in the blank and cash it in.

I thank God that He is our Provider. We can come to Him in faith, praying in the name of Jesus, and experience the rain of heaven flooding our souls. Our dry, parched ground will spring to life and we will prosper. There will be no more famine!

Praise the Lord!

CHAPTER 4

GOD'S DEBT-FREE PLAN

One of the foremost issues we face in our world is the increasing problem of debt. Not just for individuals or nations, but for the Church. I am totally convinced that debt is a device of Satan to slow down the end time harvest before the coming of the Lord.

Debt has slowly intruded and sometimes threatens our very existence. However, the Word of God gives us sound answers to this issue because the Lord wants us to have the riches we need—not only for our personal use but so we can fund evangelism world-wide.

God doesn't want us to be bogged down with financial pressures. You only have to open the pages of Scripture to see this truth.

AN AMAZING REWARD

Who doesn't enjoy the dramatic story of David killing Goliath, but there's more to the account than we realize. An amazing reward was offered by King Saul to the person who could defeat and destroy this giant enemy of Israel.

Men of Saul's army asked, *"Have you seen this man who has come up? Surely he has come up to defy Israel; and it shall be that the man who kills him the king will enrich with great riches, will give him his daughter, and give his father's house exemption from taxes in Israel"* (1 Samuel 17:25).

That was quite an incentive for David.

Goliath was a Philistine, but he had a Hebrew name, *Galah*—which means "without cover," or "to make nude."

This giant had the Hebrews under his thumb. They were his captives and he had stripped them of all their power and control and were under bondage to him.

The situation was similar to how Satan operates today. He manipulates people through debt—which is a ruling spirit with the purpose of turning you into a servant.

When David stepped onto the battlefield with Goliath, he brought something very special with him.

Yes, he had God's power and guidance, but he also picked up *"five smooth stones"* from the brook (1 Samuel 17:40).

These stones had been in the brook for a long time and had been made smooth by the rushing water.

Water represents the Holy Spirit—which God will use to polish and refine our rough edges and prepare us for a mighty assignment.

FIVE STONES

Why were there five stones? It's a good question since Scripture tells us that David reached into his bag, put one stone into his sling, and that first stone hit the giant in the forehead and killed him instantly (verse 50).

What about the remaining four stones?

Well, the giant had four sons who also needed to be vanquished. Scripture tells us, *"These four were born to the giant in Gath, and fell by the hand of David"* (2 Samuel 21:22).

David could have used anything to slay Goliath, but in the Bible we read that those who blaspheme God were to be killed by stoning (Leviticus 24:10-16).

This young shepherd boy had the anointing and the power of the Holy Spirit—the same mighty power you can use to destroy the giants you face.

I want to share five stones you need to start using in your financial life. They will release you from bondage.

Stone #1: Know that God wants you to be free of debt.

Since we serve a debt-cancelling Lord, and He is no respecter of persons, He wants you financially independent.

Stone #2: Confess that you will be debt free.

Speak to your circumstances and declare that your situation will change.

Stone #3: Become a faithful tither.

The principle of returning to God what is already His is not an option, but a command of the Father.

Stone #4: Create an out-of-debt financial flow.

The Golden Rule applies to our debt—we must do unto others what we would have them do unto us.

This means we must enter into an agreement to pay what is owed.

Stone #5: Declare your debt free intentions.

Be accountable and put yourself on the spot. Tell the Lord and others that you are determined to get out of debt. When God says, "test Me" (Malachi 3:10), He means it—and He will come through for you.

These five stones should be active and part of you plan to break free from the burden and pressure of debt.

DIVINE DIVIDENDS

When David followed God's guidance and slew Goliath, he received the three marvelous rewards that were promised: (1) great riches, (2) he married the king's daughter, and (3) the entire family of David's father lived free of debt and never had to pay taxes again. They would be forever free from financial bondage.

That was a handsome reward given to a simple shepherd boy from the highest authority in the land. The signet and seal of King Saul was as good as gold.

Just as David was part of his father's house, as

believers we are members of God's family and can receive the same blessings.

What the Almighty did once, He will do again. He has the riches of this world under His control—the gold and silver in every hill is at His command.

God's supernatural debt free plan is available for you and me. All we must do is claim it in Jesus' name.

YOU WON'T COME OUT EMPTY-HANDED

Every person alive faces dilemmas and adverse circumstances. It is only natural to wonder, "Where is God? Does He know what is happening to me?"

Let me assure you that the Lord is fully aware of your situation. In fact, if you take a look at what happened thousands of years ago, this is made evident.

Long before the Israelites were taken captive by Egypt, God gave a prophecy to Abraham. One evening as the sun was setting, a deep sleep fell over him and God spoke: *"Know certainly that your descendants will be strangers in a land that is not theirs, and will serve them, and they will afflict them four hundred years. And also the nation whom they serve I will judge; afterward they shall come out with great possessions"* (Genesis 15:13-14).

This is exactly what transpired.

Much later, after Joseph died, the people of Israel who had moved to Egypt multiplied in numbers so great that they became a threat to Pharaoh. This is when they went into slavery—for 400 years as God had foretold.

If you remember, the Lord also told them they would come out of bondage with amazing wealth! You see, God is Alpha and Omega, He knows the beginning and the end.

UP—AND OUT!

In your personal struggle, the Lord has the date circled when it will end—and you will not leave empty-handed.

What a glorious pattern. He first brings you up—then He brings you out. This is what He did for the apostle Peter in the New Testament. When Peter was thrown into prison, an angel appeared to him and said, *"Arise quickly!"* When he got up, *"his chains fell off his hands"* (Acts 12:7).

Today, "get up" in your faith, in your praise, in your worship, and in you spirit. When you do, the bondage will end and you will be set free. Hallelujah!

Satan wants to hinder the flow of God's spirit in

your life, but as you dip into the waters of praise and worship, you will experience and enjoy liberty.

God told the children of Israel, "I am going to bring you out and lead you to a land flowing with milk and honey." Pharaoh thought he was in control, but the Lord knew better.

As a believer, your heavenly Father has you in a controlled environment. He has power over every force that would come against you.

SILVER AND GOLD

After the great plagues that were inflicted upon Egypt, Pharaoh finally relented and let God's people go.

The amazing part was that the Lord gave the children of Israel such favor with their enemy that they came out of their misery prospering. The Bible records how they *"asked from the Egyptians articles of silver, articles of gold, and clothing. And the Lord had given the people favor in the sight of the Egyptians, so that they granted them what they requested. Thus they plundered the Egyptians"* (Exodus 12:35-36).

When God brings you out, you will not leave empty-handed. He *"brought them out with silver and gold, and there was none feeble among His tribes"* (Psalm 105:37).

What Satan has stolen from you, God will restore. Because of what you have been going through, the Lord will bless you with His favor and you will be on your way rejoicing.

TOTAL RECOVERY!

When you look at the life of David, in many respects he was a failure. He committed adultery with Bathsheba, arranged for the murder of her husband, Uriah, and told lies. Yet, God called him *"a man after My own heart"* (Acts 13:22).

Even though David lost everything, he never relinquished his faith—and he discovered God's plan of restoration and prosperity.

The 23rd Psalm was written by David under the inspiration of the Holy Spirit because he understood God's plan for total recovery.

How was David able to say "My cup runs over" (Psalm 23:5)? There were several reasons. First, after hiding from King Saul and fearing for his life, Saul was killed in battle and David became king of all Israel. Second, David recovered the Ark of the Covenant and returned it to Jerusalem. Third, David asked God to forgive him of his sins.

What was the result? Total recovery!

The Denial

Another prime example is Peter, a disciple who was loved by Jesus. After swearing his allegiance to the Lord, when the crucifixion was near, Peter denied Christ—not once, not twice, but three times!

It was just as Jesus had told him: *"I tell you, Peter, the rooster shall not crow this day before you will deny three times that you know Me"* (Luke 22:34).

After Jesus was arrested, a woman recognized Peter around a courtyard fire and exclaimed, "This man was with Him." Peter was quick to deny her words, saying, *"Woman, I do not know Him"* (verse 57).

A short while later another person recognized him and commented, "You also are of them." Peter responded, *"Man, I am not"* (verse 58).

About an hour later, a man charged, "Surely this fellow was with Him, because he is a Galilean." Again, Peter replied, *"Man, I do not know what you are saying"* (verse 60).

When Peter remembered the words of Jesus, he began to weep bitterly. He was at his lowest ebb—but God had a recovery plan.

Triple Forgiveness

After the resurrection, on the shores of Galilee,

Jesus showed Himself to His disciples. It's a Jewish tradition that you settle differences over a good meal and when Peter saw Jesus preparing breakfast for him, he most likely wondered, "Is it possible that I have been accepted and forgiven?"

After the meal (as recorded in John 21:15-17), Jesus turned to Peter and asked, *"Do you love Me more than these?"*

Peter replied, *"Yes, Lord; You know that I love You."* Jesus said, *"Feed My lambs."*

The Lord asked him a second time, *"Do you love Me?"*

"Yes, Lord; You know that I love You," again answered Peter.

"Tend My sheep," He told him.

For the third time, the Lord asked, *"Do you love Me?"* Peter insisted, *"Lord, You know all things; You know that I love You."*

Jesus repeated, *"Feed My sheep."*

Yes, there had been three denials, but now there were three acts of forgiveness. Peter was completely restored and went on to do a great work for Christ.

HE CAME TO HIMSELF

There may be mistakes in your past that you are

not proud of. The Lord will forgive and forget your yesterday.

How can we forget the redemptive story of the Prodigal Son? This young man was raised in a wonderful family, but he longed to leave the protection of his father's house and see the world. So he went to his father and asked, "Give me my inheritance. I want to go out on my own."

Because of his personal mistakes, the son lost all he had and ended up sleeping in a pig pen. In the words of the Bible, *"He came to himself, [and] said, 'How many of my father's hired servants have bread enough and to spare, and I perish with hunger! I will arise and go to my father, and will say to him, "Father, I have sinned against heaven and before you, and I am no longer worthy to be called your son. Make me like one of your hired servants"* (Luke 15:17-19).

When his father saw him on the horizon, he told the servants, *"Bring out the best robe and put it on him, and put a ring on his hand and sandals on his feet. And bring the fatted calf here and kill it, and let us eat and be merry; for this my son was dead and is alive again; he was lost and is found"* (verses 22-24).

There was a jubilant celebration. Total forgiveness. Total recovery.

Regardless of your past, the Lord is longing to

forgive you. We serve a God of mercy—a God of the second chance.

He will restore your health, your spirit, and give you abundance.

MIRACULOUS PAYMENT OF YOUR BILLS!

One of the phrases we see repeated in Scripture is that we are to "fear the Lord." This does not speak of being frightened, rather we are to revere and honor His name and His Word.

Did you know that God promises that if we fear Him, our bills will be paid? There will be funds in our account.

Here is the promise of heaven: *"Blessed is the man who fears the Lord, who delights greatly in His commandments. His descendants will be mighty on earth; the generation of the upright will be blessed. Wealth and riches will be in his house, and his righteousness endures forever"* (Psalm 112:1-3).

Not only will you have finances, but the Lord will feed your family. *"He has given food to those who fear Him; He will ever be mindful of His covenant"* (Psalm 111:5).

What a generous, loving God of provision we serve!

I trust you are not one of those who believe that Christians are not supposed to have money. If that's your way of thinking, you are being spiritually robbed.

The Key to God's Favor

It is not God's will for you to struggle in poverty. Start praising and worshiping the One who can supply all of your needs.

When I began to understand the Word and started glorifying God my Provider, miraculous things began to happen in my life. Financial blessings started coming my way. If I bought a stock it did well. I purchased property and sold it for a healthy profit. Good investments appeared—and continue to do so on a regular basis.

I am totally convinced that God's favor is the result of daily praising, worshiping, and giving glory to the Father who wants me to be successful in all I do.

I have learned that the more I worship God, the more blessings He provides.

If you have accepted Jesus, you have a covenant with God. And if you keep the covenant of praise and worship, the Lord will put food on your table and resources in your account.

The eyes of God are searching across the land for

people to bless. After accepting Christ as your Savior and making a commitment to keep His commandments, make it a habit to worship and praise Him *continually!* In return, He will pour out His riches beyond measure.

BIBLICAL ECONOMICS

The devil knows the contents of the Bible and has launched an all-out attack trying to convince us that a rich man cannot enter heaven. He is well aware that when believers prosper they will be able to fund worldwide evangelism.

Sadly, many in the church have accepted this lie. While the Gospel is free, it takes money to spread the Good News to the ends of the earth.

The disciples of Jesus were not beggars from birth. Peter and Andrew were successful fishermen and owned many boats. James and John came from prosperous families. Matthew was a tax collector who made plenty of money from the Jews and Romans.

Jesus knew He would need funds for His ministry and had a treasury (John 13:29). In addition, He must have worn expensive clothes because at the cross the soldiers cast lots for His valuable tunic (John 19:23-24).

It doesn't make sense to listen or take advice from a person who is not successful. Would you want financial counsel from an individual who lives in poverty? I don't think so. Neither did Solomon, the richest man who ever lived. He wrote, *"The poor man's wisdom is despised, and his words are not heard"* (Ecclesiastes 9:16).

We cannot ignore the scripture that tells us, *"Those who seek the Lord shall not lack any good thing"* (Psalm 34:10).

THE RIGHT ARMOR

Satan does not want us to understand the economics of Scripture. This is why he uses the weapon of misinformation to mislead and confuse us.

Study the Word and get to know the principles of living a prosperous life. God declares, *"My people are destroyed for lack of knowledge"* (Hosea 4:6).

You must *"be diligent to present yourself approved to God, a worker who does not need to be ashamed, rightly dividing the word of truth"* (2 Timothy 2:15).

You cannot stand on the battlefield empty-handed and not equipped to fight. When you gird yourself with God's spiritual armor, *"No weapon formed against you shall prosper"* (Isaiah 54:17).

Open the pages of the greatest book ever written and become an authority on biblical economics.

TWICE AS MUCH!

Oh, how I love God's mathematics! It's all about multiplication and you can find it from the beginning. In the story of creation the words "multiply and "increase" are used again and again, and it is the Lord's divine pattern for us today.

God is not into worn-out, patched-up living where you barely scrape by. He does not want His children, representing Him as paupers.

The word "increase" is mentioned in your Bible more than 160 times. God began an endless, flowing stream of blessing that has turned into a mighty river.

Even the DNA cells the Creator placed in our bodies are designed to continually double and reproduce. What an awesome plan!

CONSIDER YOUR WAYS!

Long ago, the prophets Haggai and Zecharia were encouraging the Judean captives who King Cyrus allowed to go back to Jerusalem in 536 B.C. These people faced a desolate situation in their homeland.

Total destruction had taken place. No homes. No buildings. No temple, and no way to make a living.

They had to start from scratch and rebuild everything. However, there was one task they left undone. They did not rebuild the Temple—which represented a relationship with God. Instead, they built their houses.

You can guess what happened. Since they did not sow, they did not reap. Their money bags, had holes in them. Their crops miserably failed and there was no prosperity.

You may be faced with the same situation. You plant, but nothing grows. You lose money at every turn. The bills keep piling higher and you can never catch up.

Stop for a moment and ask yourself, "Am I like the children of Israel? Am I neglecting the things of God?"

When you make God your top priority, He will put you first.

The prophet Haggai stood before the people with this challenge: *"Consider your ways"* (Haggai 1:7).

Zechariah *"told them, "Because of the blood of your covenant, I will set your prisoners free from the waterless pit. Return to the stronghold, you prisoners of hope. Even today I declare that I will restore double to you"* (Zechariah 9: 11-12).

Think of it. A *double* return was waiting for those who would obey God.

The children of Israel finally began to rebuild God's Temple, and when they started looking after the Lord's business they began to prosper.

Today, God is asking you and I to consider our ways. When we do, He will not only restore what has been lost, He will give us twice as much!

A DOUBLE PORTION

When the prophet Elijah was about to be taken to heaven, he said to his servant Elisha, *"Ask! What may I do for you, before I am taken away from you?"*

Elisha, passionate about seeing the ministry of Elijah continue in Israel, answered, *"Please let a double portion of your spirit be upon me"* (2 Kings 2:9).

He asked and he received.

A SURPRISING CONCLUSION

From time to time open the pages of the book of Job. Here we find a righteous man who lost everything he had—his wife, his children, and his cattle. Instead of cursing God and dying, Job prayed, *"I know that You can do everything, and that no purpose of Yours can be with withheld from You"* (Job 42:2).

Job put his trust in Almighty God and remained strong and true to his Maker despite all the horrific circumstances which crushed him. God was pleased with Job's attitude and had a surprise in store.

As we read the end of the story we learn, *"The Lord restored Job's losses...Indeed the Lord gave Job twice as much as he had before"* (verse 10).

If you read the first chapter of Job you find that he owned seven thousand sheep, three thousand camels and five hundred yoke of oxen (Job 1:3).

But now he was doubly blessed. The Bible tells us that in the latter days of Job, *"he had had fourteen thousand sheep, six thousand camels, one thousand yoke of oxen"* (Job 42:12).

Plus, the Lord restored Job's family.

WHAT AN INCREASE!

God's multiplication never ends!

At the first miracle Jesus performed, He took seven water pots and produced gallons and gallons of wine for a wedding feast.

On the day of Pentecost there were 120 gathered in the Upper Room, but before the sun set, 3,000 were added to the church. That's far more than double—it is 25 times as much!

Perhaps the greatest multiplication of all was the fact that God sent His one and only Son to earth. He was the "first fruit" of millions, even billions who have accepted Christ as their Savior and will spend an eternity in heaven with Him. What an increase!

We serve a God of unlimited grace, mercy, power, and resources. Best of all, He offers unlimited forgiveness.

Your debt of sin was paid at Calvary. You are free!

CHAPTER 5

OPEN YOUR WINDOWS!

After a cold winter, when the weather starts to warm, most people give their homes a good spring cleaning. It's a time to fling open your doors, raise the windows and let some fresh air blow through.

It should be the same in our spiritual life. Often our spirit becomes stagnant and stale and we need to open our heart to a breeze from above. It's time for a new inflilling—to become fresh and renewed.

It is part of God's plan to pour out His favor on us for keeping His commands. He tells us, *"Bring all the tithes into the storehouse, that there may be food in My house, and try Me now in this [and see] if I will not open for you the windows of heaven and pour out for you such blessing that there will not be room enough to receive it"* (Malachi 3:10).

Receive Your Assignment

Years ago, I am delighted to tell you that I opened the window of my soul to the Lord and invited Jesus in. Since that time I have learned the importance of being open to His leading. I want to receive every promise and assignment God sends my way.

I sincerely believe the Lord is searching for men and women who will declare "I know my family will be saved. I know my body is healed. I fully expect my finances to increase. I believe my dreams will come to pass."

The Lord is waiting for action on our part. He declares, *"I am the Lord your God, who brought you out of the land of Egypt; open your mouth wide, and I will fill it"* (Psalm 81:10).

Communicating with God, talking about your worries and concerns, and trusting Him is an invitation for His Word to be active in you.

Hannah's Plea

Long ago, a woman named Hannah was barren and came to the Temple to pray for a child. You can read the story in 1 Samuel 1-20.

She opened her mouth and asked God to give her the desire of her heart. Hannah fully expected her request to become a reality.

The Lord was faithful, heard her cry, and gave her a son, whom she named Samuel. This is the same Samuel who became a major prophet and served God all the days of his life.

Whatever your need, never hesitate to bring it before the Father. As the psalmist wrote, *"I called upon the Lord in distress: the Lord answered me, and set me in a large place"* (Psalm 118:5 KJV).

The same God who created the sun, moon, stars—and *you*—is able to perform miracles on your behalf. He wants to bless you today so that you in turn can bless others.

FOUR STEPS TO TAKE

If it is your desire to walk in the land of milk and honey, and see the windows of heaven open, let me recommend that you do these four things:

One: Be determined to obey the commandments of God.

Here is an eternal truth: *"If you are willing and obedient, you shall eat the good of the land"* (Isaiah 1:19).

Two: Have no fear.

You are not alone. Stand on this promise: *"God has not given us a spirit of fear, but of power and of love and of a sound mind"* (2 Timothy 1:7).

Three: Know your enemy and his limitations.

Satan is the adversary God kicked out of heaven. Since Jesus came to earth to destroy the works of the devil, he holds no power over you.

Remember, *"He who is in you is greater than he who is in the world"* (1 John 4:4).

Four: Know the power of God.

Your heavenly Father is omnipotent—all powerful! He *"both raised up the Lord and will also raise us up by His power"* (1 Corinthians 6:14).

Throw your windows open wide and receive a downpour of His strength and favor.

GOD'S PATHWAY TO SUCCESS

It's fascinating to see people striving, searching, and sometimes *shoving* their way to reach the top.

Millions of dollars are spent each year to educate the mind, develop the physique, and make us look, act, talk, and walk like winners.

Each of us has our own definition of achievement. For some it is education, for others it is their financial statement, and to many it is their social status. But what does the Bible say?

If your desire is to prosper and succeed, there is only one sure plan: *"This Book of the Law shall not depart from your mouth, but you shall meditate in it day and night, that you may observe to do according to all that is written in it. For then you will make your way prosperous, and then you will have good success"* (Joshua 1:8).

Another translation reads, *"...then you will be able to deal wisely with the affairs of life."*

Yes, we live by faith, but the Word also gives us wisdom—an essential ingredient for success,

For example, you open one store and it does well. Excited, you buy three more and they fail. Could it be that you lacked wisdom in your decision making?

THE MEASURING STICK

Have you taken the time to heed God's warning signs? Have you *meditated* on the Word as the Scripture tells us to do? If a storm is brewing, you don't jump in the car and head into the wind. No, you wait for the storm to pass. That's wisdom.

Success with God cannot be measured by the worlds standards or even compared with someone else's. Spiritual well being and growth is determined by whether you are involved with God and He with you. If the Lord is leading and guiding your steps, this is what truly matters.

Others may judge you by your possessions and wealth, but the Lord looks at your obedience. How do you react when He gives you a specific assignment? It may be to teach a Sunday School class or visit a nursing home. If you respond positively, you are successful with God.

TOTAL OBEDIENCE

Smith Wigglesworth was one of the great evangelists of the last century in England. He was a plumber who had a dramatic conversion and was often referred to as the "Apostle of Faith."

One day, God told him to go to a certain street corner of a village and "stay there until I send a man to you. Talk to him and lead him to Christ."

It was four days before a gentleman stopped to talk to him, and because Wigglesworth was open to God's voice, another soul was brought into the

90

Kingdom. Obedience was the key.

The Gospel writer James said, *"Show me your faith without your works, and I will show you my faith by my works"* (James 2:18).

Being a follower of Christ is more than just sitting around repeating the words, "I believe in God." We have to *"be doers of the word, and not hearers only"* (James 1:22).

Some may say, "I'm believing the Lord for my financial success," but when the offering plate is passed they keep their money tightly folded in their pocket.

This is in direct opposition to God's law of seed-time and harvest. The Bible gives us this assurance: *"Give, and it will be given to you: good measure, pressed down, shaken together, and running over will be put into your bosom. For with the same measure that you use, it will be measured back to you"* (Luke 6:38).

I've heard the complaint, "The church is financially well off and doesn't need the small offering I can give." Wake up! It's not about the church, rather our obedience to God's Word.

BECOME "WORD CONSCIOUS"

Sadly, some people are trying to get by on the

Word they learned 5 or 20 years ago, but Scripture tells us to *"meditate in it day and night"* (Joshua 1:8). This means now—today.

Let me encourage you again to become "Word conscious" so that no matter what the situation, you can confront it with a powerful verse.

Become so saturated with Scripture that you absorb it like a sponge. If any problem touches you, the water of the Word will pour out. When you do this, the devil will run.

Remember, on the Mount of Temptation, Jesus defeated Satan with the Word! So can you!

THE POWER TO GET WEALTH

Prosperity is not about possessions, it is about priorities. It's about obedience to God's Word.

Praise the Lord! I have read my Bible and know my rights. I have a covenant that has been stained by the blood of Jesus, Without question I have what is required to prosper financially.

Here it is in black and white: *"You shall remember the Lord your God, for it is He who gives you power to get wealth, that He may establish His covenant which He swore to your fathers, as it is this day"* (Deuteronomy 8:18).

Let me encourage you to read this scripture again

and again and commit it to memory.

When the terrorists hit the World Trade Center towers they could have flown those planes into Hoover Dam or any army base in the country. Why the Trade towers? They represented the financial center of the world. It was all about money.

Satan and his misguided followers crave the wealth of the nations, but they don't understand the power to *get* wealth. Please hear me when I repeat that the prosperity message is not a money message—it is all about obedience.

A DIVINE PARTNERSHIP

It's foolish to think of God as an unapproachable deity floating in the far beyond, looking down on us with a furrowed brow, waiting for us to make a mistake so He can dispense punishment.

This is far from the truth. He desires to be closer to you than you can ever imagine.

Here are the words of Jesus: *"I am the vine, you are the branches. He who abides in Me, and I in him, bears much fruit; for without Me you can do nothing"* (John 15:5).

How close is a branch to the vine? Since one is an extension of the other it is often impossible to tell where the branch starts and the vine ends. One fact is certain: the branch continually draws nutrition from the vine. A separation would result in death.

This parallels our partnership with God. It is a bond that produces abundance. In this passage Jesus explained, *"If you abide in Me, and My words abide in you, you will ask what you desire, and it shall be done for you"* (verse 7)

One of the life-altering days of your journey will be when you stop working *for* God and begin working *with* God.

IN PERFECT SYNC

Your heavenly Father is not just some "big boss" in the sky, who encourages and supports "little old you" toiling down here on earth. He's not the main speaker at a rally who turns you loose to go out and do His work. No, the Lord actually goes with us. He is our partner and we are always in His presence—which never changes.

You may question, "Can I have contact with God all the time? Can I keep Him always on my mind?"

Yes. This is the relationship Jesus had. *"Most assuredly, I say to you, the Son can do nothing of Himself, but what He sees the Father do; for whatever He does, the Son also does in like manner"* (John 5:19).

He further stated, *"I do not seek My own will but*

the will of the Father who sent Me" (verse 30).

How close was the partnership? In the words of Jesus, *"I am in the Father and the Father in Me"* (John 14:11).

Jesus was in perfect sync with His Father. I thought about this when I was speaking through an interpreter in Central America. When I moved, he moved. When I gestured, so did he. When my voice became louder, his did too. We were as one.

UNBROKEN COMMUNICATION

As you read the story of Lazarus, you learn his family was grieving because the man had died. When Jesus heard the news He announced, *" This sickness is not unto death, but for the glory of God, that the Son of God may be glorified through it"* (John 11:4).

Jesus could be that intimate with God because He had unbroken communication with His Father. This kind of relationship is possible for us because as believers, *"For whom He foreknew, He also predestined to be conformed to the image of His Son"* (Romans 8:29).

We are closer to the Lord than we realize. *"Do you not know that your body is the temple of the Holy Spirit who is in you, whom you have from God, and you are not your own?"* (1 Corinthians 6:19).

The Spirit of God is not only *with* you but *in* you. His presence is permanent and always available.

A Covenant Relationship

Our partnership with the Almighty is often described as a marriage—which requires honest, ongoing communication. Have you noticed that couples who live together a long time often begin to sound alike, walk alike, and think alike. They can usually finish each other's sentences.

This is how it should be as we take God as our partner. His thoughts and ways become ours. We take on the heart of the Father in a covenant relationship with Him.

Remember, *"It is He who has made us, and not we ourselves; we are His people and the sheep of His pasture"* (Psalm 100:3). A good shepherd never abandons his sheep.

Let me encourage you to read Psalm 139 as often as you can. In it we find these inspiring words:

O Lord, You have searched me and known me. You know my sitting down and my rising up; You understand my thought afar off. You comprehend my path and my lying down, and are acquainted with all my ways.

For there is not a word on my tongue, but behold, O Lord, You know it altogether. You have hedged me behind and before, and laid Your hand upon me. Such knowledge is too wonderful for me; it is high, I cannot attain it.

Where can I go from Your Spirit? Or where can I flee from Your presence? If I ascend into heaven, You are there; if I make my bed in hell, behold, You are there. If I take the wings of the morning, and dwell in the uttermost parts of the sea, even there Your hand shall lead me, and Your right hand shall hold me.

If I say, "Surely the darkness shall fall on me," even the night shall be light about me; indeed, the darkness shall not hide from You, but the night shines as the day; the darkness and the light are both alike to You. For You formed my inward parts; You covered me in my mother's womb.

I will praise You, for I am fearfully and wonderfully made. Marvelous are Your works, and that my soul knows very well. My frame was not hidden from You, when I was made in secret, and skillfully wrought in the lowest parts of the earth. Your eyes saw my substance, being yet unformed. And in Your book they all were written, the days fashioned for me, when as yet there were none of them. (Psalm 139:1-16).

What a glorious description of the presence of God.

GIVE HIM EVERYTHING

I once heard the following and have never ever forgotten it:

1: Give God all your *waking* thoughts. Before you face the day face the Father. Begin your morning with prayer.

2: Give God all your *waiting* thoughts. He wants us to be still and know that He is God—listen as He speaks to you.

3. Give God all your *whispering* thoughts. Practice brief sentence prayers every two or three minutes. When you stop at a red light, wait in a drive-in window, or stand in line at the bank, take a moment to pray. This is how we *"pray without ceasing"* (1 Thessalonians 5:17).

4. Give God all your *waning* thoughts. At the end

of the day let your mind settle on God. Fall asleep talking to the Father.

As you take God as your partner and spend time in His presence, there will be less and less of you and more and more of Him.

You will be forever changed. The glow of His glory will shine on your face. You will truly be the branch of His vine.

LIVING THE ABUNDANT LIFE

The devil is out to rob and ruin your relationship with the Lord, but the everlasting Peacemaker came to give us the abundant life.

Scripture makes this clear: *"The thief does not come except to steal, and to kill, and to destroy. I have come that they may have life, and that they may have it more abundantly"* (John 10:10).

This confirms that through the Son of God, not only can we be saved but we can prosper—in health, in joy, in finances, and look forward to an eternity in heaven.

When you click on the television, the world would have you believe that the "good life" is a couple strolling down a sandy beach with a can of beer in their hands. They try to convince us, "It doesn't get much better than this."

Nothing could be further from the truth. You can never find happiness or abundance in a bottle, a pill, drugs, or sex—only through Christ Jesus.

Satan paints an enticing picture of fame, money, or political power, but be aware: his real plan is to destroy you.

The route we choose is ours.

The Final Question

One of the keys to the abundant life is service.

I once met a young doctor who gave up his thriving practice to serve as a medical missionary in South America. To him, ministry was far more important than money.

When we stand before the final judgment, the Lord will not question you about your education, your career, or your finances. He will ask, "What have you done for Me?"

The Lord wants to know if you helped those in need—the stranger, prisoner, those less fortunate. Jesus is saying, *"Inasmuch as you did it to one of the least of these My brethren, you did it to Me."* *(Matthew 25:40)*.

Abundance also grows out of service to your local congregation. If you profess to belong to a church but don't attend, it's a lie. According to the Bible we must not abandon *"the assembling of ourselves together"* (Hebrews 10:25).

In addition, abundant living means separating yourself from the world and surrounding yourself with people of faith.

Speaking of those who believed on His name, Jesus said, *"I have given them Your word; and the world has hated them because they are not of the world, just as I am not of the world"* (John 17:14).

Finally, abundant living encourages an intimate relationship with the Lord. This means, prayer, Bible study, and finding God's purpose for your life.

A DOOR NO MAN CAN CLOSE

At this very moment, Jesus is opening up marvelous doors for you—ones of blessing, provision, and opportunities for rich spiritual growth and service.

He declares, *"I have set before you an open door, and no one can shut it"* (Revelation 3:8). He also holds the keys to hell and death (Revelation 1:18).

The entrance to the prosperous life is before us and all we have to do is take a step of faith and walk inside. It is your passage to salvation, healing, and financial blessings.

The invitation has been given and now it is up to you. *"The Spirit and the bride say, 'Come!' And let*

101

him who hears say, 'Come!' And let him who thirsts come. Whoever desires, let him take the water of life freely" (Revelation 22:17).

God not only opens doors, He opens eyes. After the resurrection, as Jesus was eating with His disciples, *"Their eyes were opened and they knew Him"* (Luke 24:31).

As you study the truth of God's Word, ask the Lord, *"Open my eyes, that I may see wondrous things from Your law"* (Psalm 119:18). This was the cry of the apostle Paul when he was in prison. He requested prayer *"that God would open to us a door for the word, to speak the mystery of Christ, for which I am also in chains"* (Colossians 4:3).

That door has been opened for you and me. It is the entrance to abundant living.

Are you ready for God to shower you with favor beyond measure?

It's time to live the prosperous life.

PART II

...AND BE IN HEALTH

CHAPTER 6

GOD'S HEALING COVENANT

In our culture, the word "miracle" has become a mere figure of speech. We talk about "miracle drugs, "miracle soap, "The Miracle on the Hudson, and a "miracle home run" to win the baseball World Series.

However, if you really want to see the supernatural at work, open your Bible and read about the parting of the Red Sea which allowed the children of Israel to cross on dry ground—or how Jesus fed 5,000 people with one boy's small lunch. Now those are miracles!

This brings us to the second part of our foundation scripture: *"Beloved, I pray that you may prosper in all things and be in health, just as your soul prospers"* (3 John 1:2).

A BOND FOR BELIEVERS

The Lord wants you to be healthy and whole— even if it takes an intervention from heaven. As we will learn, our physical well being is part of a divine covenant God has made for you and me. It is His nature:

- God made a covenant with Noah that he and his family would be saved in the devastating flood (Genesis 9:8-17).
- God made a covenant with Abraham that He and his seed would produce a mighty nation (Genesis 12:1-3; 17:2).
- God made a covenant with David to make him Israel's greatest king and that through his lineage would come the Savior (2 Samuel 7:8-16; Psalm 89).
- God made a new covenant for New Testament believers—including you and me (Matthew 26:26-28; Hebrews 8:8-13).

Healing and health are central to the bond the Lord has made with all believers. It is how God deals with the sickness and disease that came to mankind after the fall of Adam and Eve in the Garden of Eden. They were filled with fear and were cursed by God (Genesis 3:10,14).

A HOLY ORDINANCE

Disease is one of humanity's greatest enemies, yet long ago, the Lord established an ordinance that provides protection for us.

When the children of Israel were in the wilderness, after the miracle of the bitter waters being made sweet, God established *"an ordinance for them, and there He tested them, and said, 'If you diligently heed the voice of the Lord your God and do what is right in His sight, give ear to His commandments and keep all His statutes, I will put none of the diseases on you which I have brought on the Egyptians. For I am the Lord who heals you'"* (Exodus 15:25-26).

This scripture is not a design of Abraham, Isaac, Jacob, Moses, Aaron, Joshua or Caleb. It is God's plan. When we turn to the Lord in repentance, He hears and answers prayer.

Jesus dealt with sickness and disease from the beginning of His ministry. In the very first sermon He preached after He was baptized and tempted by Satan, Jesus proclaimed, *"The Spirit of the Lord is upon Me, because He has anointed Me to preach the gospel to the poor; He has sent Me to heal the brokenhearted, to proclaim liberty to the captives and recovery of sight to the blind, to set at liberty those who are oppressed; to proclaim the acceptable year of the Lord"* (Luke 4:18-19).

From that point forward, Jesus traveled through Judea preaching the Kingdom and healing the sick and oppressed.

Every miracle had the backing of the Word of God. This was according to Scripture: *"He sent His word and healed them, and delivered them from their destructions"* (Psalm 107:20).

THE FULFILLMENT

We must understand that the miracles of Jesus were performed under the old law. However, He stated, *"Do not think that I came to destroy the Law or the Prophets. I did not come to destroy but to fulfill"* (Matthew 5:17).

When the rich young ruler asked, "What must I do to be saved," Jesus told him to keep the commandments. That was the old covenant. Today, we have the new covenant which was prophesied long ago: *"Behold, the days are coming, says the Lord when I will make a new covenant with the house of Israel and with the house of Judah"* (Jeremiah 31:31).

Today, our salvation and healing is based on the

work of Calvary. *"He was wounded for our transgressions...and by His stripes we are healed"* (Isaiah 53:5).

Thousands of years before, in the wilderness, the children of Israel began to grumble and complain against both God and Moses. So the Lord sent fiery serpents among the people; many were bitten and died.

Then God instructed Moses, *"Make a fiery serpent, and set it on a pole; and it shall be that everyone who is bitten, when he looks at it, shall live"* (Numbers 21:8).

Moses did as the Lord commanded and those who looked on the pole with the serpent attached were healed.

This is prophetic because Jesus became sin on the cross (a pole or a tree). He bore our sins and the stripes He took provides our healing.

THE COMMISSION

The Creator of the universe had a plan for our salvation and healing that was implemented before the foundation of the earth. He knew that His Son must come to be our substitute.

The Hebrew noun *rachamin* and the Greek word *eleeo* both are translated mercy and compassion—and this is what Jesus demonstrated to those in need.

After His ministry of miracles, the Lord commissioned His disciples to *"Heal the sick, cleanse the lepers, raise the dead, [and] cast out demons"* (Matthew 10:8). Again, He said His followers would *"cast out demons....they will lay hands on the sick, and they will recover"* (Mark 16:17-18).

Later, when He sent out the 70 to minister, they returned with amazing stories of miracles, exclaiming, *"Lord, even the demons are subject to us in Your name"* (Luke 10:17).

The commission of Christ is to all who believe —and has never been revoked.

This passage of Scripture is relevant for us today: *"Is anyone among you sick? Let him call for the elders of the church, and let them pray over him, anointing him with oil in the name of the Lord. And the prayer of faith will save the sick, and the Lord will raise him up. And if he has committed sins, he will be forgiven. Confess your trespasses to one another, and pray for one another, that you may be healed"* (James 5:14-16).

The thread of healing has run through the ages. The psalmist wrote, *"Bless the Lord, O my soul, and forget not all His benefits: who forgives all your iniquities, who heals all your diseases"* (Psalm 103:3)

The Son of God is still our healer.

IS IT GOD'S WILL?

Some ask, "Isn't disease a curse?" It may be, but *"Christ has redeemed us from the curse of the law, having become a curse for us"* (Galatiians 3:13).

I've also heard both men and women confess, "I don't believe it is God's will to heal me."

Those who pray, "If it be Thy will," cancel out the Word. There is no "if." Scripture is the revelation of God's will and when He promises healing, that is what He does.

Faith rests on your knowledge of God's will and the work of healing is done when your will meets His. Keep claiming this promise: *"If you abide in Me, and My words abide in you, you will ask what you desire, and it shall be done for you"* (John 15:7).

Healing is yours!

THE GIFTS

Every claim of healing you make is fully covered by God's Word—what an incredible insurance policy that is. You don't ever have to pay a premium and there are no deducible clauses. It is completely free!

The working of miracles is one of the spiritual "power gifts" available to believers *now.* They include, *"gifts of healings...[and] the working of miracles"* (1 Corinthians 12:9-10).

The Bible does not say that we will all have every gift; they are distributed *"to each one individually as He wills"* (verse 11). However, they are all supernatural.

BEYOND MEDICAL SCIENCE

A man named Luke wrote both the books of Luke and Acts. He accompanied Paul on several missionary journeys. Once, they were shipwrecked on Malta and invited to stay at the home of a man named Publius. Scripture records that the man's father *"lay sick of a fever and dysentery. Paul went in to him and prayed, and he laid his hands on him and healed him. So when this was done, the rest of those on the island who had diseases also came and were healed"* (Acts 28:8-9).

Luke, a medical doctor by profession, was present, but no where do we read of him giving a diagnosis or a prescription. While the knowledge of doctors is a gift from God, it is no match for the supernatural.

The reason Jesus could heal and cast out devils is because *"God anointed [Him] with the Holy Spirit and with power, who went about doing good and healing all who were oppressed by the devil, for God was with Him"* (Acts 10:38).

That same anointing is available to all who call on His name.

THE GREAT PHYSICIAN

At the age of ten I was supernaturally healed of hepatitis C with yellow jaundice. It had infected my liver, which was swollen and about to burst. Doctors were saying that I would soon die.

My mother laid hands on my stomach and prayed. When she did, a light filled the hospital room and I received a miracle. I went home—totally healed!

Many years later, when I began to teach and preach on the subject of healing, I was not conscious of any special gift or manifestation. But as I laid hands on the sick and asked God to heal them—He did!

I have been praying for people in the name of Jesus ever since.

In the Panama Canal Zone, I shared my testimony and asked men, women, and children to come forward for prayer. The first woman told me through the interpreter that she had a bleeding ulcer. I anointed her with oil and prayed, then went on to the next person.

Suddenly, I turned around and saw the first woman vomit up the ulcer on the floor. She was totally healed by the power of God. I had never witnessed anything like that before in my life.

After many years of ministry I have seen too many miracles to count—crossed eyes straightened, deaf ears unstopped, arthritic hands made whole, and so much more.

Our God is the Great Physician!

"I Shall Not Die"

Nothing is more devastating than to hear a doctor utter the words, "You have cancer"—an aneurysm, or any life-threatening condition. When some individuals hear such a report they lose all hope and start planning their own funeral.

This is not the time to throw in the towel. Instead, stand to your feet and declare, *"I shall not die, but live, and declare the works of the Lord"* (Psalm 118:17).

Do you have a battle plan against sickness and disease? Take courage in the fact that *"The Lord is a man of war"* (Exodus 15:3), He is ready to fight by your side.

You can wage the battle for your healing:

- Through praise (Psalm 63:3-4).
- Through confession (Psalm 107:20).
- Through resistance (James 4:7).
- Through singing (Acts 16:25).
- Through forgiveness (Psalm 103:2-3).
- Through fasting (Mark 9:28-29).
- Through prayer (James 5:15).

You have help. The Lord will send angels—His heavenly air force—to fight for you.

Because of God's covenant, you have authority over sickness and disease. Claim it in the name of Jesus.

CHAPTER 7

GOD'S MEDICINE BOTTLE

I have nothing against doctors—in fact I have great respect for the profession and have made many visits to their offices over the years. After their exams and diagnoses, before I leave there is one last step they usually take. You probably know what that is. They write out a prescription for me to take to a pharmacist and have filled.

The doctor says, "If you take these pills I think you'll get better."

This is a huge and profitable business. The international drug companies have worldwide sales of over $300 billion annually.

However, I want to let you in on a secret. I know a source for the best prescription in the world—and it's absolutely free!

God has made available to us the medicine of His Word which relieves our pain and heals every illness.

LIFE AND HEALTH

There is a powerful passage of Scripture I referred to in chapter 2 that I want you to look at again—especially since it concerns your healing. It is God's perfect prescription for you. *"My son, give attention to my words; incline your ear to my sayings. Do not let them depart from your eyes; Keep them in the midst of your heart; for they are life to those who find them, and health to all their flesh. Keep your heart with all diligence, for out of it spring the issues of life"* (Proverbs 4:20-23).

The word *"flesh"* speaks of your total physical body. If you have faith for the healing of every inch of you—inside and out—there will be no room for sickness to reside in any part of your being.

God is talking about His Word being *"life"* and *"health"* to *"those that find"* it.

This means more than simply reading; we have to take action and find what He has prescribed. Even more we have to follow the directions.

When you read the label on the bottle of pills your doctor has asked you to take, you'd better follow the instructions exactly as written. If it tells you to swallow two pills every night, that doesn't mean one at supper and the other at breakfast.

There are four specific directions God is giving us in these verses:

Number 1: "Give attention to my words" (Proverbs 4:20).

There comes a time when we must stop talking and start listening. This is especially true when God speaks—He requires our undivided attention.

It's amazing how young people can have music blaring in the background, the television set on full blast, all while they are trying to do their homework! We could call this, "divided attention disorder."

The Lord is asking us to focus and zero in on His Word—it is the key to biblical healing.

Here are the rules and the results: *"If you diligently heed the voice of the Lord your God and do what is right in His sight, give ear to His commandments and keep all His statutes, I will put none of the diseases on you which I have brought on the Egyptians. For I am the Lord who heals you"* (Exodus 15:26).

Number 2: "Incline your ear" (Proverbs 4:20).

The definition of the word "incline" is to bend down—which means you have to lean forward, almost bowing. This is a sign of humility.

I've listened as parents correct their children with the words, "Don't argue with me." In God's sight, we are the pupils and He is the teacher—and we'd better listen!

When Stephen, the follower of Christ, was brought before the religious council, he charged them as being *"stiff-necked...in heart and ears!"* (Acts 7:51).

Even today, some people, due to their background, prejudice or preconceptions have mental barriers when it comes to scriptures which relate to God's power to heal.

They need to incline their ear, because *"faith comes by hearing, and hearing by the word of God"* (Romans 10:17

Receive your healing with a spirit of meekness.

Number 3: "Do not let them depart from your eyes" (Proverbs 4:21).

"Them" refers to the words of the Lord as written in Scripture. We need to open our Bible and see the truth with our own eyes. However, when it comes to spiritual matters, many of us suffer with blurred vision.

Jesus taught, *"The lamp of the body is the eye. Therefore, when your eye is good, your whole body also is full of light. But when your eye is bad, your body also is full of darkness"* (Luke 11:34).

It is the Lord's desire to bring health to your whole body—and when you are filled with the Light of Christ, there is no room for sickness.

To those who obey the Word, *"The Sun of Righteousness shall arise with healing in His wings"* (Malachi 4:2).

Taste and "see" that the Lord is good.

Number 4: "Keep them in the midst of your heart" (Proverbs 4:21).

Your physician may tell you that for certain medicines to be effective, the active ingredient has to enter the blood stream.

The purpose of having God's Word enter through the ear gate and the eye gate is so it reaches your heart. This is why we are told, *"Keep your heart with all diligence, for out of it spring the issues of life"* (Proverbs 4:23).

If your heart is made perfect, your life will be too.

The scalpel of a surgeon can cut deep into human tissue, but what the Lord says reaches areas left untouched by mortal men: *"For the word of God is living and powerful, and sharper than any two-edged sword, piercing even to the division of soul and spirit, and of joints and marrow, and is a discerner of the thoughts and intents of the heart"* (Hebrews 4:12).

121

If you have a disease in the bone, there is often no human medicine that can adequately deal with it. This is also true of many inner personality problems that no psychiatrist can solve.

Thank God, His Word is sharp and penetrates—to your very heart.

HE HEALED THEM ALL

It is not the desire of your heavenly Father to see just some of His children healed—but *all* of them.

You may say, "That's impossible. Some—but not all!"

We should not doubt or argue with Scripture. The New Testament is filled with stories of individuals who were healed and delivered by Jesus and His disciples. However, there were thousands of additional miracles which were not recorded.

In the city of Capernaum, after delivering a demon possessed man in the synagogue and healing Peter's mother-in-law, *"When the sun was setting, all those who had any that were sick with various diseases brought them to Him [Jesus]; and He laid His hands on every one of them and healed them"* (Luke 4:40)

Not just two or three, but every single one!

THE MULTITUDES

It is recorded that after Jesus healed a man with a withered hand, *"Great multitudes followed Him, and He healed them all"* (Matthew 12:15).

This scene happened again at Gennesaret where they *"brought to Him all who were sick, and begged Him that they might only touch the hem of His garment. And as many as touched it were made perfectly well"* (Matthew 14:35-36).

After Jesus ascended to heaven, the disciples continued His ministry of miracles. Immediately following the Upper Room experience, many signs and wonders were taking place. At one point, *"a multitude gathered from the surrounding cities to Jerusalem, bringing sick people and those who were tormented by unclean spirits, and they were all healed"* (Acts 5:16).

In God's vocabulary, all means all!

SPEAK FAITH!

It's time for believers to remove the barriers that restrict them from receiving God's miracle touch. For many, this means guarding our tongue.

I've heard even God-fearing men and women say,

"It's flu season and I always get sick." "My mom had cancer and I suppose I will have it too." Even worse, "This curse has been on my family for years. There's nothing I can do about it."

These individuals need to start practicing the principles of the Word and start speaking faith. *"Death and life are in the power of the tongue"* (Proverbs 18:21).

Do the words you utter bring sickness or blessing? The Bible tells us: *"Fight the good fight of faith, lay hold on eternal life, to which you were also called and have confessed the good confession in the presence of many witnesses"* (1 Timothy 6:12).

Speaking faith will deliver us from the deadly conditions of this sin-cursed world. It enables us to receive God's promises and be connected to His favor.

Your faith will be unshakable when you know His promises. Tell that headache to leave your body now—talk to your disease in the name of Jesus.

"By His Stripes"

The next time sickness strikes, instead of relying only on a penicillin or flu shot, take a "spiritual shot" of Scripture.

I know a man who had cancer and repeated, "By His stripes I am healed" over 1,000 times. He told me,

"Every time I said those words my faith continued to grow." The power of God flowed into his body until the cancer totally left him.

Instead of inviting failure, start thinking like your heavenly Father: *"For My thoughts are not your thoughts, nor are your ways My ways,' says the Lord. 'For as the heavens are higher than the earth, so are My ways higher than your ways, and My thoughts than your thoughts'"* (Isaiah 55:8-9).

It's time to tell the demons of sickness to flee!

WORSHIP AND WELLNESS

There is not one weakness, disease or defeated moment that has ever come from God. He knows no defeat, no sickness, no pain.

Regardless of what you may be going through, start worshiping the Lord. Since *"every good and every perfect gift is from above"* (James 1:17), stay in close fellowship with Him.

Satan must never be allowed to distract you from lifting your hands and praising the One who loves you. That's what the devil would have you avoid—especially since he was a praise and worship leader in heaven and knows the power it brings. But he was thrown out of the Kingdom because he wanted to be like God (Isaiah 14:13-14).

His downfall was that he stopped bowing down to the Almighty.

No matter what your accomplishments—if you have built a dozen churches and have led multitudes to Christ—if you stop worshiping the Lord you will not only lose your vision but separate yourself from the God who heals.

If you are sick in body, you have the only prescription that never fails. Read and delight in His Word—it will bring life and health to your flesh.

CHAPTER 8

THE MIRACLE MAN

I was preaching at a church in Alabama when a young man, about 26 years old, came forward to be prayed for.

I learned later that he was a former football player for Auburn University. He was a big, strapping fellow—six feet five, weighing about 240 pounds. He was married to a beautiful woman and they had two lovely children.

"What would you like me to pray with you about?" I asked him.

He responded, "I have an enlarged heart and the doctors tell me I could die at any minute." He was on the hospital transplant list to receive a new heart.

I asked him, "Do you believe that God is going to heal you right now?"

"Yes I believe," he confidently said. There was no hesitation in his voice.

I laid my hands on his head and prayed, "In the

name of Jesus, God heal this man for Your glory. Make his heart perfect in size and function. Heal him and anoint him for Your service."

This happened on a Wednesday night. Two days later he went back to the hospital for his weekly checkup. When the doctors looked at the x-ray and MRI scans they were buzzing and called for more consultants to come and take a look. They were amazed at what they saw!

The young man knew what had happened. No more enlarged heart. No more talk of a transplant. God had healed him.

OPERATING IN THE ANOINTING

As I study the gospels of Matthew, Mark, Luke, and John, no matter what miracle Jesus was performing —whether it was casting out devils, healing or forgiving men and women of their iniquity—none was more difficult than the other. It was just as easy for the Lord to say "Take up your bed and walk," as "Your sins are forgiven."

You see, the Son of God was operating in the anointing of His heavenly Father and through the power of the Holy Spirit.

The most significant fact is that He is still the worker of miracles. The same Jesus who healed the woman with the issue of blood will heal cancer today.

Just one word from the Man of Galilee and the cripple walk, the dumb talk, and blind eyes are opened.

If we are having trouble seeing results, the problem is not with Jesus—it is with us. We are not putting our total trust in Him and believing His Word.

He Spoke Healing

Early in His ministry, Jesus returned to the village of Cana, near Galilee, where He had performed His first miracle—turning water into wine.

There He was approached by a nobleman whose son was very sick in Capernaum. The man had heard that Jesus was nearby so he sought Him out and pleaded for Him to come and heal his dying son.

Jesus turned to the nobleman and said, *"Unless you people see signs and wonders, you will by no means believe"* (John 4:48).

Once more the man begged, *"Sir, come down before my child dies!"* (verse 49).

Jesus told him to go on his way because his son

would be just fine. There was no need for Jesus to go to the man's home—He simply spoke healing.

With great faith, the nobleman believed what the Lord told him and the next morning he headed to his home. On the way his servants came running to greet him with the good news, *"Your son lives!"* (verse 51).

On the spot, the jubilant father asked his servants to tell him the exact hour his boy had recovered. They replied, *"Yesterday at the seventh hour the fever left him"* (verse 52).

It was the same moment that Jesus told him his son would live. The man and his entire household believed on Jesus.

JUST ONE WORD

All you need is a word from heaven!

One morning, when Jesus was at Galilee, a large crowd gathered to hear Him teach. About the same time, He saw two boats on the shore, but the fishing crew had gone off to wash their nets. So the Lord stepped into one of the vessels and asked Peter to row out a little distance from the land and there He began to speak to the multitude.

When He had finished, he turned to Peter and

said, *"Launch out into the deep and let down your nets for a catch"* (Luke 5:4).

Peter resisted, telling the Lord they had fished all night and caught nothing.

What Peter said next turned the entire situation around: *"Nevertheless at Your word I will let down the net"* (verse 5).

That was all Jesus needed to hear: "At Your word!"

They caught so many fish their nets were breaking. In fact, they signaled to their partners in the other boat to come and help them. They filled both boats so full *"that they began to sink"* (verse 7).

When you act on orders from the Lord, you will experience a miracle catch!

ONLY A TOUCH

In a village of Judea lived a woman who had an incurable disease. For 12 years she had been hemorrhaging with an issue of blood. We are not told, but it could have been a bleeding cancer.

One thing we do know: it could not be cured. She had been to many doctors and spent all her money in the process. Still, her condition worsened.

The woman was at the point where she realized

that she was beyond human hope. This is when fear and panic sets in.

About this time, the stories of a miracle worker reached her. She heard that a prophet, a rabbi, was traveling throughout Judea healing the sick and bringing peace to their souls.

Crowds were always pressing Jesus from all sides; He hardly had time to eat or sleep, or reach out to so many in need. But the word spread that if they could only touch the hem of His garment, they would be healed.

This was the first ray of hope this woman could cling to. She stopped thinking about the doctors, the loss of her money, or past failures. Instead, she dreamed, "If He can do that for other people, He will do it for me."

A SURGE OF HEALING

On the day Jesus was to pass through her town, all her plans were laid aside. She was not a spectator standing on the sidelines waiting to see what all the commotion was about. This woman had one objective—to make contact with Jesus.

The crowd grew and the disciples were trying to help the Master move through the excited throng.

Somehow, she inched closer and closer. Then she reached out her trembling hand and grabbed the hem of His robe.

Every time I read this story I am reminded of Jacob who wrestled with an angel all night thousands of years before. The angel finally said, *"Let me go, for the day breaks"* (Genesis 32:26). But Jacob replied, *"I will not let you go until you bless me."* (verse 26).

When this persistent woman touched His garment, it must have been like putting her fingers on a live electrical wire—of course, there was no such in those days.

The effect, however, was still the same. Suddenly, the healing power of Christ surged through her body. Every fiber of her being was affected—and in an instant she was cured of her disease. Not only was her hemorrhaging healed, so was her entire body, mind, and spirit.

At that moment, Jesus, *"knowing in Himself that power had gone out of Him, turned around in the crowd and said, 'Who touched My clothes?"* (Mark 5:30).

The disciples had no idea what had just taken place. They responded, *"You see the multitude thronging You, and You say, 'Who touched Me?'"* (verse 31).

Inner Peace

When Jesus turned around He saw the woman, *"fearing and trembling, knowing what had happened to her"* (verse 33).

Scripture tells us that she fell before Jesus and told Him the whole story. He looked at her, saying, *"Daughter, your faith has made you well. Go in peace, and be healed of your affliction"* (verse 34).

Jesus gave her more than healing in her body; He gave her inner peace.

We are never told the woman's name—perhaps so we could put our name where her's would have been. Whatever your need, He wants to do the same for you.

Today, we do not need to touch a piece of clothing to release our faith. It is as simple as believing that Jesus is our healer.

Was This the Messiah?

The Son of God wants you to prosper and be in health physically, mentally, emotionally, and spiritually.

Scripture tells us, *"Jesus went about all Galilee,*

teaching in their synagogues, preaching the gospel of the kingdom, and healing all kinds of sickness and all kinds of disease among the people" (Matthew 4:23).

He healed:

- Those with leprosy (Matthew 8:2).
- The demon possessed (Matthew 8:16).
- A paralytic (Matthew 9:6-7).
- The blind (Matthew 9:29).
- The deaf (Matthew 7:32).
  - and so many more.

The Jews in the days of Jesus were not surprised by miracles. They had been part of the history of Israel—being led by a cloud and fire, the parting of the Red Sea, the walls of Jericho falling down, and the wonders of Elijah and the prophets.

However, when they heard that the daughter of Jairus and Lazarus had been raised from the dead, they hardly knew what to think.

Was this a man sent from God, or a false prophet? So the religious leaders started to look for any excuse to pour scorn and ridicule on Him. They could not comprehend that this could possibly be the long-awaited Messiah.

The matter came to a head at a gate near the pool

of Bethesda (which means "house of compassion"). The people thought the waters had special powers.

A severely disabled man, who could hardly move, was lying there. He had been lame for 38 years.

When Jesus saw him in that condition, He asked, *"Do you want to be made well?"*

The man thought someone had come along to help him into the waters, but instead, Jesus commanded, *"Rise, take up your bed and walk"* (John 5:8).

Immediately, the man was healed, picked up his bed, and began to walk.

MIRACLES EVERY DAY

Upon hearing what had happened, the Jews were outraged. Why? Because nothing like this was to occur on the Sabbath. The Bible records, *"For this reason the Jews persecuted Jesus, and sought to kill Him, because He had done these things on the Sabbath"* (verse 16).

Jesus was not caught off guard, He knew exactly what He was doing. He was determined to destroy their idea of what should or should not take place on this Holy day.

Scripture chronicles that Jesus healed on the Sabbath seven times:

1. The man at the pool we have just mentioned (John 5).
2. The man born blind (John 9).
3. The demonic (Mark 1:21-28).
4. Peter's mother-in-law (Mark 1:29-31).
5. The man with the withered hand (Mark 3:1-6).
6. The stooped woman (Luke 13:10-12)).
7. The man with dropsy (Luke 14:1-6).

When it comes to miracles, God has no Sabbath —He will heal you any day of the week.

Right now, no matter what situation you face, the Lord is saying, *"Do not be afraid; only believe"* (Mark 5:36).

Jesus is the Miracle Man!

CHAPTER 9

TEN STEPS TO HEALING AND HEALTH

Years ago, a young Irishman dreamed of coming to America, the land of hope and promise. He finally saved the money for the fare, but not enough to pay for his meals aboard the ship. He did, however, manage to scrape up a few coins for a bag of cheese and some stale bread to carry him through the long voyage.

One evening, after several days at sea, the Captain was walking along the deck and noticed the man near the bow, eating his cheese and bread. "Why aren't you in the galley eating with the other passengers?" he asked.

"Sir," he answered," I only had enough money for the passage, but not enough for my meals."

The Captain was delighted to tell him, "Son, didn't

you know that when you bought your ticket your meals were included with your fare?"

Just as the young man was unaware his meals were a benefit that was paid for in the price of his ticket, there are many believers who seem oblivious to the fact that Christ's atonement on the cross paid for blessings in addition to salvation and eternal life.

Never forget the words of this verse: *"Bless the Lord, O my soul, and forget not all His benefits: who forgives all your iniquities, who heals all your diseases"* (Psalm 103:2-3).

Since the days of the Old Testament, the Lord has always desired to see His people free from sickness and disease—from cancer to the common cold.

This became clear during the earthly ministry of Jesus, when He spent so much of His time healing those who were sick.

Since we know that it is the will of God for us to prosper and be in health, let me share ten steps to receiving your healing:

Step #1: Recognize that sickness and disease is the oppression of the devil.

Because of the fall of man in the Garden of Eden, sin and sickness entered this world. And even though

God allows disease and illness on this planet, its source is not our heavenly Father, but the devil.

This truth is evident when we read: *"Satan went out from the presence of the Lord, and struck Job with painful boils from the sole of his foot to the crown of his head"* (Job 2:7).

Illness is simply not God's nature. *"Every good gift and every perfect gift is from above"* (James 1:17).

Remember that Jesus *"went about doing good and healing all who were oppressed by the devil"* (Acts 10:38). Satan attacks human life, but Jesus is a destroyer of the works of the evil one.

Step #2: Believe God will heal you.

There are many who go around saying, "Yes, I believe God *can* heal me." However, the statement we need to make—and mean it from the depths of our being—is: "I believe God *will* heal me!"

Belief and miracles are linked together. The Roman centurion whose servant was lying at home, paralyzed, had total belief that Christ could perform a miracle. Jesus recognized this and said to him, *"'Go your way; and as you have believed, so let it be done for you.' And his servant was healed that same hour"* (Matthew 8:13).

How strong is your belief?

Step #3: Understand that healing begins in the inner man.

When the Creator breathed life into Adam, he *"became a living soul"* (Genesis 2:7 KJV).

Today, you reach out to God and God reaches you through your soul. As the strings of an instrument respond to the touch of human fingers, your body responds to the impressions of your soul.

Our most severe struggle lies within us. Tension, insecurity, and fear are symptoms of sickness and in order to be healed, there must be peace in our soul and spirit.

Healing starts with a change on the inside—then God's power will begin to flow through your body.

May you be *"strengthened with might through His Spirit in the inner man"* (Ephesians 3:16).

Step #4: Claim the promises of God's Word.

It is the will of the Father for you to be healed, but until you claim what God has promised, they are simply words on paper. Memorize specific verses and keep them in your heart and on your lips:

- *"I am the Lord who heals you"* (Exodus 15:26).
- *"He sent His word and healed them"* (Psalm 107:20).
- *"By His stripes we are healed"* (Isaiah 53:5).
- *"I will restore health to you and heal you of your wounds"* (Jeremiah 30:17)."
- *"Let us return to the Lord...He will heal us"* (Hosea 6:1).
- "*He...took our infirmities and bore our sicknesses"* (Matthew 8:17).

Step #5: Release your faith.

I've heard people actually say, "I will be healed when God is ready."

The Lord is *always* ready—He is waiting for us to release our faith and believe Him for the answer this very minute.

To the leper in Samaria, Jesus commanded, *"Arise, go your way. Your faith has made you well"* (Luke 17:19).

What was the Lord looking for? Faith!

What was true in Bible days is still true today: *"The prayer of faith will save the sick, and the Lord will raise him up"* (James 5:15).

Step #6: Go where the power is.

If you were looking for physical help, would you seek out someone who was weak and frail? No. You would find a person who is strong and has plenty of muscles.

I am happy to report that the Healer we serve has unlimited might. Yes, *"The Lord God Omnipotent reigns!"* (Revelation 19:6).

Jesus knew the source of His miracle ministry on earth. He declared, *"All power is given unto me in heaven and in earth"* (Matthew 28:18 KJV).

Everywhere He went, there were wondrous works taking place because, *"The power of the Lord was present to heal them"* (Luke 5:17).

If you are searching for divine answers, go were the power is.

Step #7: Lose yourself in God.

How can we expect miracles if we try to keep pace with a hectic world and delegate no time to spend in God's presence?

Find a quiet place to be alone with the Great Physician. Shut yourself away from any commotion or confusion—and stay there until you meet the Lord and

He meets you. Be still and know that He is God (Psalm 46:10).

Lose yourself in the Lord!

Step #8: Find a point of contact.

Since the Son of God is in heaven, how do we reach Him? It is through a point of contact. This includes reading His Word and releasing our faith, but there are also other ways He reaches out to us.

In the New Testament, there are many instances where healing took place by the laying on of hands. This happened often in the ministry of Jesus (Mark 6:5; Luke 4:40; 13:13).

As believers, we have been given authority to do the same: *"They will lay hands on the sick, and they will recover"* (Mark 16:18).

God uses many instruments to touch lives. In the days of Peter, they brought the sick into the streets and his very shadow brought healing (Acts 5:14-15). And during the ministry of the apostle Paul, *"handkerchiefs or aprons were brought from his body to the sick, and the diseases left them"* (Acts 19:12).

Today, radio and television is being used as a contact point for God's healing power. All of these can increase our faith and bring us closer to the Healer.

Step #9: Join yourself to companions of faith.

If you want to see your prayers multiply, lock arms with those who know the Lord and stay close to Christians who will join you in prayer. Stay in an atmosphere of God's love and don't allow anyone to steal your faith.

Jesus said, "*If two of you agree on earth concerning anything that they ask, it will be done for them by My Father in heaven. For where two or three are gathered together in My name, I am there in the midst of them*" (Matthew 18:19-20).

The word agreement in Greek is "symphony"—like a find-tuned orchestra. When we unite in faith, the Lord is present.

Step #10: Take authority over sickness and disease.

As followers of Christ, we have been given the right to represent Him on this earth and take charge. We can't afford to back down.

Jesus took command of every situation. He would loose the ears of the deaf and they would hear. He would straighten the legs of the cripple and they would begin to walk. To a man with a demon spirit,

Jesus demanded, *"Come out of him!"* (Luke 4:35). Instantly, the demon left.

The virtue of healing and deliverance flowed from the Lord like a pure mountain stream, and the same authority has been given to you and me: *"Whatever you bind on earth will be bound in heaven, and whatever you loose on earth will be loosed in heaven"* (Matthew 16:19).

When you act on the words of Jesus, your own words will take on new power!

The Word of God is not only for a chosen few; it is for you. Today, stand and declare, "I *will* prosper—I *will* be in health!"

PART III

...As Your Soul Prospers

CHAPTER 10

THE KEY TO
THE KINGDOM

I heard the story of a six-year-old boy who was talking with his great-grandfather, who was 84.

"Grandpa, how old are you," the youngster asked.

His answer startled the boy. "Son, I am only four years old."

"You've got to be kidding me. I know you're a lot older than that," responded the disbelieving grandson.

It was a teaching moment for the old man concerning salvation when he explained, "You see, four years ago I gave my heart to Jesus and I was born again. For the first 80 years I just existed, but when I got saved, I really began to live."

He was an example of a great Bible truth: *"If anyone is in Christ, he is a new creation; old things have passed away; behold, all things have become new"* (2 Corinthians 5:17).

Eternal Prosperity

In God's Kingdom the number three is significant. We find examples of it over and over again:

- Father, Son, and Holy Ghost
- Body, soul, and spirit
- Spirit, water, and blood
- Abraham, Isaac, and Jacob
- Peter, James, and John

In our foundation scripture there are also three separate elements. It speaks of our prosperity, our health, and our soul. *"Beloved, I pray that you may prosper in all things and be in health, just as your soul prospers"* (3 John 1:2).

Many only focus on the first two—and ignore that the key to every blessing from above is having a prosperous soul.

Yes, it is awesome to have material welfare, but it is limited to our time on this earth. *"For we brought nothing into this world, and it is certain we can carry nothing out"* (1 Timothy 6:7).

However, spiritual prosperity is eternal. When God speaks of your soul, He is talking about *"the life that now is and of that which is to come"* (1 Timothy 4:8).

WHERE IS YOUR TREASURE?

By giving your heart and soul to the Lord you will experience eternal health and prosperity. This is why Jesus tells us: *"Do not store up for yourselves treasures on earth, where moth and rust destroy, and where thieves break in and steal. But store up for yourselves treasures in heaven, where moth and rust do not destroy, and where thieves do not break in and steal. For where your treasure is, there your heart will be also"* (Matthew 6:19-21).

There are many ways to "pay ahead"—by helping those in need with no ulterior motive and by being generous and kind. But there is not a specific list of "good works" that will unlock the gates to an eternity in heaven. It takes more than personal effort; it requires forgiveness of sin.

THE TRANSFORMING PLAN

When a religious leader named Nicodemus came to Jesus with words of flattery and praise, the Lord changed the course of the conversation and told him: *"Unless one is born again, he cannot see the kingdom of God"* (John 3:3).

Nicodemus was confused and wondered how a

man could be born when he was old. *"Can he enter a second time into his mother's womb and be born?"* (verse 4).

Jesus explained, *"Unless one is born of water and the Spirit, he cannot enter the kingdom of God. That which is born of the flesh is flesh, and that which is born of the Spirit is spirit. Do not marvel that I said to you, 'You must be born again'"* (verses 5-6).

In this same conversation, Jesus presented the plan of salvation that has transformed millions of hearts and lives through the centuries: *"For God so loved the world that He gave His only begotten Son, that whoever believes in Him should not perish but have everlasting life"* (John 3:16).

Without asking Jesus to be your personal Lord and savior, you are merely existing instead of experiencing the abundant life.

WILL YOU PRAY WITH ME?

If you have never given your heart to Christ, I invite you to pray this with me:

Dear God, I know that I have sinned and that my sins separate me from You. I am truly sorry. Please forgive me.

I believe that Your Son, Jesus Christ, died for

my sins, that He was raised from the dead, is alive, and hears my prayer.

I invite Jesus to become my Savior and the Lord of my life, to rule and reign in my heart from this day forward and forever more. I pledge to grow in grace and knowledge of You.

My greatest purpose is to follow Your example and do Your will for the rest of my life. And I pray this in the name of Jesus.

Amen.

If you meant these words from the depths of your heart, I want to welcome you to the family of God.

All the promises of the Father are yours. You will truly know what it means to prosper and be in health—because your soul has prospered.

Praise the Lord!

NOTES

For Books and Media Resources
or to Schedule the Author for Speaking
Engagements, contact:

Tommy Combs
Healing Word
Living Word Ministries
P.O. Box 1000
Dora, AL 35062

Phone: 1-866-391WORD (9673)
Internet: www.tommycombs.org
Email: tommy@tommycombs.org